NEW
PARADIGMS

FOR
CREATING QUALITY
SCHOOLS

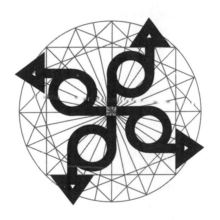

BRAD GREENE, ED.D.

FOREWORD BY WILLIAM GLASSER, M.D.

Cover design by Paul Turley
Text Layout by Douglas Gibson & Dixon Smith

ISBN 0-944337–23–6

Library of Congress Catalog Card Number: 94–069069

Quantity Purchases
Companies, professional groups, clubs and other organizations may qualify for special terms when ordering quantities of this title. For ordering information contact the Sales Department, New View Publications, P. O. Box 3021, Chapel Hill, NC 27515-3021.
1-800-441-3604

Contents

Dedication

In loving memory of my father, Don Greene, and to my mother, Doris Greene, who for over fifty years modeled what a quality relationship should look like, and what is more important, the skills and commitment necessary to make it grow and endure.

And to my wife, Donna, who for over thirty years has given me the love, support and encouragement to put in writing my experiences in public education. For the past three years in my full-time consulting in education across the United States and Canada, she has been my business partner and best friend. She has accompanied me, sharing with others our ideas and experiences in this never-ending, continuous journey to improvement and quality. She enhances the quality of my life each day with her love, acceptance, and desire to grow and improve in these concepts, and with the kind, gentle, giving spirit that she shows when interacting with the many wonderful people we meet in our consulting across our nation.

Acknowledgments

I am most grateful to Dr. William Glasser for his guidance, support, patience, and friendship. Dr. Glasser challenged my thinking as together we led the staff and students of Apollo High School to apply the concepts and principles that led towards quality. Even though Apollo has a long way to go, we definitely made a good beginning and are continuing to make progress on the journey to quality.

I owe thanks to many individuals: To the many fine faculty members in Dr. Glasser's Institute for Quality Management who, by their own lives and modeling of "quality concepts," have taught me so much and enriched my life. A special thanks to Kathy Curtiss who has served as my mentor and friend and taught me the principles of quality through her teaching and by example. To Bob Hoglund, who worked so hard with the Apollo staff and me and by his patience and skill brought us along on the journey to improvement. To Jeanette McDaniel, a senior faculty member with the Institute, who played a key part in my training to be certified as a faculty member. I could not have asked for a better model of these concepts than Jeanette, a truly quality teacher. And to Linda Harshman, director of the Institute and faculty member, who by her teaching and encouragement helped me through the process. To Perry Good, faculty member and author, who provided guidance, support, and encouragement throughout the process of writing this book. Without her help I would have given up at those times when I could not see the light at the end of the tunnel. To John Kohlmeier who not only provided me with excellent suggestions but did much editing along the way. John is not only a friend, but also a good example of a quality teacher. All of my three children had the honor of being his students, and to this day they state that John was one of the best teachers they had during their public school experience. To Nancy Salmon, who helped me with the struggle of going from lecturer to writer.

Lastly, thanks go to the 300 school districts I have had the honor to work with during the past three years in my new capacity as a full-time quality school trainer. You have taught me a great deal by your willingness to be "risk takers" and by your efforts to implement these new paradigms in your programs. The stories and examples of your successes are important contributions to this book. You have proven that internalizing these quality principles in our own lives is the most important factor in facilitating them to become a reality in the lives of our students. You have proven that these paradigms do work, that they improve the quality of our lives and our schools.

Foreword

The major obstacle to learning is fear: fear of failure, fear of criticism, fear of appearing stupid, fear of speaking up, fear of risking, fear of trying, fear of disapproval, fear of letting others down, and even the fear of succeeding. We must establish conditions in which it is safe for students to risk making mistakes. A quality teacher makes it possible for each student to err with impunity. To remove fear is to invite effort. To welcome mistakes is to encourage learning. To establish trust is to create a sense that I care: I am here to help you, not to hurt you; I have your best interest in mind. When you achieve, do quality work, and meet your needs, then I, too, do the same. Whether we build a climate of trust or fear will determine if we do quality work or work that is "just good enough."

The most important skill required to create this type of environment is the ability to manage others. This long needed book describes clearly what Brad Greene did when he decided to try to move the Apollo School to a Quality School. As principal, Brad demonstrated the management style and skills needed to create quality schools that I call lead management. Apollo moved a long way, perhaps not all the way to becoming a Quality School. I have no doubt that had Brad remained at Apollo, the school would have gone all the way.

Since he joined me in 1991 as a full-time Quality School consultant and trainer, Brad has reached many teachers, administrators, board members, and superintendents. Because of Brad's insights into the Quality School concepts, his understanding of control theory, and his experience at Apollo, many other schools are now moving towards becoming Quality Schools. The role of school leader is vital, for if he or she does not actively lead in the way described here, nothing significant will happen. *New Paradigms for Creating Quality Schools* is a book about the dedication and skills needed, the hard work involved, and the satisfaction of seeing students being successful and doing quality work. If you are interested in the specifics of turning your school into a Quality School, READ THIS BOOK!

William Glasser, M.D.
November, 1994

Preface

In 1987, Dr. William Glasser began working with the staff and students of Apollo High School in southern California, where I was then serving as principal. He was the first consultant to build credibility with our teachers by demonstrating on a one-to-one basis the success you could have with his ideas about quality schools.

In the past we had tried many different staff-development programs, and we had sincerely tried to implement what we learned in these programs, but nothing seemed to stick for more than a year or so. Now I know why. All of these programs were the creations of someone else. They dealt primarily with ways to improve teachers, or ways to make students conform, become better learners, or ways to correct their misbehavior. Dr. Glasser taught us new paradigms. Their impact on our school was tremendous. He taught us that the lack of quality work was not the fault of people, staff, students, or parents, but rather, the problems were within the system. The key to change was a massive paradigm shift.

A paradigm is a mental model of how things work in the real world—it is, in a sense, a "best guess" based on experiences we have had and information we have received. Our beliefs, values, and actions are shaped by our paradigms. As we receive new information, however, our paradigms can change, and when that happens, our thinking and behavior are likely to change as well. Consider, for example, the revolutionary paradigm shift that led to the

American system of democratic government. For many centuries a predominant paradigm in western Europe was that some individuals are inherently superior to others by virtue (or accident) of their birth. This paradigm was the underpinning of government by monarchy, a rigid class system, inheritance by primogeniture, etc. "All men are created equal" is a contrasting paradigm which, once adopted, led many people to flee Europe for America, to the writing of the Declaration of Independence, to government headed by an elected president and legislature with defined terms, universal public education, etc.

It is sometimes difficult to identify the paradigms which guide our thinking and our actions, but examining our paradigms can pay great dividends. When things are not working out as well as one would like, it is tempting to blame someone or something for the problem. We say, "If only I (or someone else) could work harder, do something differently, could do it better....then all would be well." The problem, however, is often not the effort, skills, nor intentions of the people involved, but the paradigms on which their actions are based. If we are able to get people to change their paradigms, we usually find that their actions, beliefs, and values change too. A paradigm shift has a cascade effect—one thing leads to another.

Dr. Glasser helped us learn to see things in a different way and adopt new paradigms so that our attitudes and our behavior changed, thus leading to increased quality in our relationships, the school environment, and the students' school work.

Chapter 1

From Good Enough
to Quality

Too often school administrators and teachers concern themselves with what is "good enough." What score is "good enough" for passing a test? Is the term paper "good enough" for an A? B? C? How many credits are "good enough" for graduation? With so many educators busily defining minimum levels of competency, perhaps we shouldn't be surprised that many students barely attain, much less surpass, the low levels of achievement on which so much attention is focused. On the other hand, if students set their sights on excellence, the chances are good that they will end up with quality results. Striving for quality is a bit like preparing to jump over a hurdle—one shouldn't worry about jumping just "high enough" when there is no danger of jumping too high. By aiming for the best, you insure that "good enough" will take care of itself.

Critics frequently denounce public schools for failing to graduate literate, skillful, responsible citizens who are well prepared for future employment or the rigors of college, but few educational reforms have generated long-lasting or widespread improvements. The Quality School movement, however, shows much promise. It was initiated by psychiatrist Dr. William Glasser, who became a leader in educational reform with the publication of *Schools Without Failure* (1969) and later *The Quality School* (1990). Already well known for reality therapy, an effective counseling technique, Dr. Glasser combined principles of control theory with Dr. W. Edwards Deming's insights on quality to argue for the creation of a school environment very different from the familiar one—an environment in which the focus is on quality work, discipline is maintained without coercion, and students continuously evaluate their own work.

The changes needed for a school to move from "good enough" to "quality" are numerous and substantial. How can it be done? People cannot really be taught how to change by other people. Suggestions can be offered. Ideas can be given. Strategies can be shared. Training can be done. But someone else's program cannot be copied in order to become a quality school. Change requires a decision that comes from within each person, and decision makers at each school must create their own path for their journey toward quality.

Everything is created twice. First is the mental creation, then the physical creation. If we are not a part of the mental creation, we are unlikely to be committed to the physical creation. The involvement, commitment, and ownership we need to discover quality comes from both creations. If we are not a part of both, it just will not work. When you create involvement and ownership, you establish commitment and pride, and out of pride comes quality.

When Dr. Glasser began working with us, Apollo High School was considered about average for a school serving mostly "at-risk" students. Daily attendance hovered around seventy-two percent of enrollment. Achievement test scores were low. Costs to repair vandalism were high. Tardiness, poor behavior, and substance abuse were frequent problems. Some students were on probation for criminal activity. Many of the students came from dysfunctional families. Most who did their school work were doing just enough to get by.

After four years, during which Dr. Glasser taught us the new paradigms that create Quality Schools, the picture had changed considerably. Attendance reached ninety-four percent. The school's yearly cost for vandalism had dropped to one of the lowest in the district. Scores on state achievement tests increased forty-nine percent in the areas of math, reading and writing—the biggest improvement of any school in Ventura County. The frequency of tardies and many discipline problems declined. The dropout rate fell, and the number of students graduating and going on to further education increased. Many students were beginning to do "quality work" instead of "it's good enough the way it is" work. Teachers were becoming involved in school improvement.

While working as a consultant for the past few years, I have seen many other schools successfully adopt Quality School principles. These schools, at all levels from primary grades on up, have experienced significant improvements in achievement, discipline, and morale.

Step one in the transformation to a Quality School is accepting that if we want quality we have to focus on it. Students and staff must discuss it, define it, learn how to recognize it. Quality must become part of the school's mission. This is not a one-time event—there is no definition to memorize quickly. Discussions of quality should occur frequently—in classes, in staff meetings, among students, teachers, and others. At Wheatland High School (Wheatland, Wyoming) the teachers meet weekly to discuss quality school issues and share their discoveries. Wheatland High School also holds monthly meetings for parents to learn about quality school concepts, ask questions, and express concerns about the process. Such organized opportunities for discussion help the entire school community to focus on quality.

The important thing is to have students and staff discuss quality frequently. What characteristics are associated with quality? Is there a difference between quality and quantity? What are the barriers to quality? Particular emphasis should be on what quality looks like, what it feels like, and where we now have quality in our lives. Gradually, a sense of quality and desire for quality develops.

In the Edina Public Schools (Edina, Minnesota), student forums were organized at three levels: fifth grade (elementary school), sixth to ninth grades (middle school), and tenth to twelfth grades (high school). A week before the forums were scheduled to occur, students received copies of potential questions to be discussed, along with the invitation to ask other questions related to quality, school improvement, and effective learning. Although questions for each level differed slightly, they included such ideas as: How do you know when you do good work? What makes a good class? In what class or activity are you putting forth your best efforts? Why? Do grades reflect your learning? Why or why not? How is your school supporting and encouraging you to learn? What does your school do well? How could your school be improved so you could learn better?

Insights gleaned from students during the discussions included: They learn best when they are actively involved in the learning process. They enjoy a variety of tasks and working in groups. They put forth more effort when they are challenged, when what they learn is interesting, and when they see that learning is important. They see good teachers as caring, friendly, enthusiastic about teaching, good at communicating, fair in their evaluations, and holding high expectations. They said that teachers' comments on their assignments told them more about the quality of their work than did the grade they received. In general, the students' responses were closely related to the characteristics of a quality school identified by Dr. Glasser (1990, 186-190).

Key questions that we asked Apollo students to get them discussing quality are listed in Figure 1. Similar questions are the basis of an exercise that can be done with students in groups of three. Each student takes a role—reader/summarizer, timer/recorder, or spokesperson. For thirty minutes the members of each group discuss the specific questions until they agree on definitions. Then they share their definitions with other members of the class. As the teacher writes the various definitions of quality on the chalkboard, the students discover common elements and similarities.

For quality to flourish, coercion must be eliminated. Dr. W. Edwards Deming insists that it is impossible to produce a quality product as long as fear exists, but a tremendous amount of fear exists in schools today. Teachers can reward or punish students and they often use this coercive power, causing fear. Quality relationships are never built upon fear. Instead, they are supportive, caring, and friendly. In working toward quality one must learn principles of management based on an understanding of basic human needs and internal motivation so that one acts as a "leader" instead of a "boss." To accomplish their goals, leaders involve others in planning and decision-making, thus creating commitment, unlike bosses who rely on coercion and thus engender fear.

The third critical element of a quality school program is to have students evaluate their own work. Over the years I have found that students rarely resist efforts to focus on and talk about quality, and they favor reducing coercion, but they often resist efforts to get them to make self-evaluations. The process itself does not intimidate them as much as what they find out when they evaluate their own work. Many students have said, "If I have to start evaluating my own work, I am going to have to work a lot harder." No one wants to evaluate himself as inferior—and that is exactly why we want students to become self-evaluators. Self-evaluation is a skill. If learned in school, it can be used for the rest of one's life to improve the quality of life.

Are you one of those people who think "quality" means "expensive"? If so, you are mistaken. One of Dr. W. Edwards Deming's principles of quality is that it saves money! The Japanese, who embraced Deming's teachings after World War II, demonstrated this principle with their successful automobile industry. As we moved toward quality at Apollo High School, we generated savings in several ways.

The state of California provides approximately $4,000 per student for their educational costs for a school year, calculated as a daily amount (ADA) of approximately $23 times 180 school days. When students are suspended, the school is not reimbursed for the ADA during their absence. During the year before Dr. Glasser began working with us, our suspensions ran about 14 percent of the student population. As we improved our communication skills and learned reality therapy (parts of the quality school training), suspensions decreased to less than one percent, gaining us more than $11,000 a year from additional ADA's. For four years we had the lowest number of suspensions among the eight secondary schools in our district.

California schools also do not receive the ADA for days when a student's absence is unexcused. We had been averaging about twenty-five percent absenteeism each day. To solve this problem, teachers changed their methods so that students perceived what they were learning in class was useful, and students began calling other students who were absent, trying to get them to come to school. They even made home visits when they were not getting results on the phone. Attendance went from seventy-five percent of our student population to ninety-two percent the first year, to ninety-six percent the second, third and fourth years, and our income increased by $98,000. During this period, due to the funding problems in our district, we had to cut two of our three counselors and a teaching position. The additional ADA money allowed us to make our half-time counseling position full time, and we were able to replace the lost teaching position.

Previously, vandalism was costing us $8,000-$12,000 a year. As we moved toward quality, the students began to take pride in how the campus looked and accept responsibility for its appearance. They painted murals, re-decorated restrooms, and worked with teachers to beau-tify classrooms with wallpaper, wood panels, fresh paint, etc. People take care of what they have had a part in cre-ating and designing. In a period of one year, our vandal-ism costs decreased to less than $500. The savings were more than enough to pay all the costs for the quality school training we did at Apollo.

The teacher and students in a photography class, in discussion with their parents, designed a project that taught students how to transfer 8mm movies from film to video-tape. For a very nominal fee parents could send in their old family movies and have them transformed into videos. Some of the earnings were used to fund a field trip for photography students to visit Brooks Institute in Santa Barbara where they observed and talked to professional photographers. In doing the project, the students had learned a skill which enriched their lives and those of others, and they earned money for a trip that otherwise would have been impossible because the district budget had eliminated field trips.

A school in Fort Collins, Colorado, whose staff was working on quality, saved more than $10,000 in one year by reducing the amount of copying teachers did. As teachers improved the quality of their lessons, they used fewer learning packets which asked students to fill in the blanks. The money saved was used in more exciting and useful ways.

Together the staff and students of Copperas Cove High School (Copperas Cove, Texas) set a goal for energy conservation that generated savings of $3,500 in one year. This school also attracted community volunteers to tutor students and to supervise hallways, which reduced the need for additional paid staff.

These are just a few of the many ways quality schools can find to improve the "bottom line." Quality saves money, it doesn't cost money!

The remaining chapters of this book explain the key paradigm shifts which spur the transformation to becoming a quality school. The book does not attempt to be a comprehensive explanation of how it was done in any one place, because each school staff in its quest for quality needs to create its own process guided by the key paradigms described here. The examples and anecdotes have been drawn from numerous schools throughout the country. The challenge is to create change from within the system, with individuals at each school defining what they need to do to transform the status quo into a process of continuous improvement, a journey toward quality.

Figure 1

Questions for Discussing Quality

1. What is your definition of quality?
2. What adjectives would you use to describe quality?
3. How do you recognize quality?
4. What kinds of quality are there?
5. What is the relationship between quantity and quality?
6. What are some of the indicators of quality?
7. Give some personalized examples of quality work. How did you know it was quality?
8. How has producing quality work helped you? How has it hurt you?
9. What facilitates quality work and/or products? What hinders it?
10. Quality in school:
    What is quality in teaching and/or administration?
    Give two examples of quality on your campus.
    Who should determine whether school work is quality?

Chapter 2

From Busy Work
to Quality Work

Before exerting maximum effort on assignments, most young people must be convinced that what they are being asked to learn has some relevance to their present or future lives. For some, it may be sufficient to know that it must be learned to pass the test, to get a good grade in the course, or to build a strong transcript so they can attend the college of their choice. For many others, however, the material must be more immediately useful and practical or they couldn't care less.

Lesson structure and the learning process in which students engage strongly influence how well they will grasp the desired knowledge and master the skills. Unless the lessons actively involve them, the students will have difficulty retaining and applying the material. As one quality teacher remarked, "My goal is to have the students work harder than I do!"

A quality curriculum focuses more on the skills that students need to develop than on the facts they need to know, although subject matter and skills are closely intertwined. One cannot practice learning skills without having some particular subject matter to be learned. To stimulate learning activity, it helps to have significant, meaningful information to work with, but many alternative choices for subject matter are possible. Once individuals have become "skillful" learners, they will be prepared and able to acquire any particular knowledge they deem necessary or interesting.

There are three general methods by which students learn—the "tell me" method, the "show me" method, and the "involve me" method. With the "tell me" method, students forget 90 percent of what they heard within a day. A U.S. History teacher, using the tell-me method, lectures the students about each of our forty-two presidents, from first to last, and asks the students to memorize the names of the presidents in the order they were elected and certain facts about each one. An objective test asks them to regurgitate what they have been told. Even if they successfully memorize everything they are supposed to for the test, we know that within a very short time they will forget nearly all of it.

With the "show me" method, visual information is provided as well as auditory, but learning is still essentially a passive process and about fifty percent is forgotten within a week. Watching demonstrations and videos are common examples of show-me learning. The history teacher, above, using the show-me method instead of tell-me, might present information about the presidents in a slide show so the students could see as well as hear what they were going to be asked to memorize. As with the tell-me method, long-term retention is poor.

Real learning takes place by the "involve me" method. People learn much more when they participate actively in learning. For involve-me learning, students might present a drama, conduct a science experiment, or build something. People retain about 90 percent of what they learn at the involve-me stage. To get students to learn about presidents at the involve-me level, the history teacher might ask students each to choose five presidents to study and show them how to do research. He might then ask the students to describe to the class what each of their five presidents would be remembered for and answer such questions as: Describe four or five problems that existed in the country during each president's term. How did he try to solve those problems? Do any of those same problems still exist today? If you were president, how would you deal with these problems?

There is an old proverb that states, "Tell me, and I'll forget. Show me, and I may remember. Involve me, and I'll understand." The Cone of Learning (Figure 2) illustrates the three levels of learning as they are related to the level of involvement.

Most teachers are familiar with the six steps of learning that have come to be known as Bloom's Taxonomy—Knowledge, Comprehension, Application, Analysis, Evaluation, and Synthesis. The six levels of Bloom's Taxonomy do not mean a great deal, however, until they can be described as specific skills by which students learn. Figure 3 describes the six levels of Bloom's Taxonomy and identifies nine skills under each by which students can demonstrate their understanding of the information and show how they are using it. If we can take knowledge and information and help students to convert it into a specific skill, then the student is learning at the involve-me stage. What is desired in a quality school is to design lessons and learning activities at the involve-me stage.

Remember, in a quality school the knowledge and information that comes from the real world must go into the perceived world of the students' minds. Then it must go through the filtering process whereby students evaluate whether the knowledge would be useful in their lives now and in the future. In some very tangible way, they must see how this learning will add quality to their lives and maybe even the lives of others.

As a guideline for quality education, the Apollo School adopted recommendations from a report that appeared in the *Association School Curriculum and Development Journal* in December 1989. Personnel directors from companies across the United States had been interviewed about what skills students should have in order for them to be considered desirable potential employees. They identified seven key skills or traits. First, students have to know how to learn. Companies expect to train new employees in how to build their product or provide their particular service, but a company should not be responsible for teaching the basic skills needed for a student to be successful in a job training program. Currently companies spend $35 billion a year providing remedial education to new employees before they can train them, according to *The Learning Gap* (1992) by Harold Stevenson. Second, students need skill in listening, and third, in oral communication. Fourth, employable students need competency in reading, writing, and computing. Fifth, incoming employees need to be adaptive. Companies value employees who have creative thinking and problem solving skills. Sixth, employees need to have personal management skills. They should be able to set goals and be motivated to reach their goals. They should have some idea where they are going in their career. Seventh, new workers need to be able to work effectively in groups. Interpersonal skills are critical components of teamwork. Inability to get along with others is a major reason why employees are terminated from companies. At Apollo we began discussing how we could create specific academic outcomes that would demonstrate the students' competency in these seven areas. Students understood that they would have a better chance of getting a job if they learned these skills and could demonstrate them to others.

Some English teachers in Tyler, Texas, created a Scholars Program for students who desired to improve their qualifications for university entrance and college scholarships. The program, which averages about ninety students each year, focuses on skills needed for taking college entrance tests, such as the SAT, and for getting better grades. The number of students entering four-year colleges such as Harvard, Princeton, Duke, Rice, MIT, UCLA, and the Air Force Academy, has increased. The average gain in SAT scores for the group was more than 100 points. Before the program began, about four percent of students received college scholarships, but twenty-one percent of students earned scholarships after being involved in the program. The key to these impressive results is the effort expended by the students when they recognized and accepted the clearly defined goal of college entrance which made the various learning activities meaningful.

Let me now describe some specific examples of quality learning activities. These are only a few of the possible ones I could recount. I am sure you can think of many from your own experience as well. Look for the common threads—meaningful material, useful skills, active student participation. They are all involve-me activities.

To improve their writing skills, one teacher at Apollo High School required her students to write three letters: a personal letter to whomever they wanted, a letter of introduction which was essentially a one-page resume, and a letter of persuasion on any topic they wanted to get others to see from their point of view. As students wrote their letters, evaluated them, and made improvements, they began to realize the better the quality of their letters, the better their chances of passing the final test, which was not of the traditional sort. To pass the test for the personal letter, the school mailed the letter and the student had to get an answer. To pass the test for the resume, the student had to show it to an employer in the community who verified that it was well written. The letter of persuasion had to be published. As students wrote and rewrote their letters, they gained competency in writing. Later they moved on to writing short stories.

For another example, during the Clinton-Bush election campaign a social studies teacher brought in videos of CNN, NBC and CBS polls and then discussed with the students how people conduct polls to find out what various voters are thinking before they cast their votes. The teacher suggested that the students conduct their own polls. Groups of five students came up with ten questions they all agreed on and that each would be willing to ask twenty-five people in their neighborhood. Each group conducted its poll and reported back to class. The class was surprised to find that fewer than fifty percent of the people they interviewed were intending to vote. Most students knew a person had to be eighteen years old to register to vote, but it turned out that only one of nine eighteen-year-olds in the class had registered to vote. That student explained to the rest of the class how to register to vote. Then the teacher had a voter registrar come into class to register those students who wished to vote in the next election and to explain how they could vote by absentee ballot if they were going to be out of town. Afterwards, some of the students went back to the people they polled who were not going to vote and told them what they had learned about registering to vote and getting absentee ballots. With this new information, half of those who had originally not intended to vote changed their minds!

Several students who were tutoring in an elementary school while also enrolled in a wood-construction class at Apollo High School were asked by their supervising elementary teacher if they could build playhouses for kindergarten/first-grade classrooms. The children could bring in empty milk cartons, cereal boxes, and other things to fill up the shelves with "merchandise" and pretend to be going to a real grocery store, or they could pretend the playhouse was a post office, with the children play-acting how they would mail letters and buy stamps or be a postman.

The students interviewed their "customers" to find out what it was they were looking for in their playhouse, then drafted architectural plans for the custom houses. They learned mathematics and measurement skills as they developed the plans and translated the plans into structures. They practiced many different building techniques.

Working together in teams, they learned how to cooperate. As a result of continuously self-evaluating their product, they eventually built excellent-quality playhouses. Some were waterproof to be used outside. Some had shutters, screens, Dutch doors, windows and shelving. Some were even paneled and carpeted. The students developed great pride in a job well done.

At Washougal High School (Washougal, Washington), one requirement for graduation is that each senior must complete a written research project under the mentorship of someone in the school or community and present the project to a panel of faculty and community people. Students are involved in selecting both the projects and the mentors with whom they will work. They must use at least five resources and self-evaluate their progress as they make revisions and improvements until they feel ready to make the final presentation. Examples of past projects include building a fiberglass boat, a project on search and rescue, shadowing an engineer for a week at the Boeing aircraft plant in Seattle, and participating in a leadership seminar on decision-making skills given at a local company. The projects have had such a positive effect that students in lower grades are asking to do similar, smaller-scale projects to prepare themselves for their senior project.

The 125 students of a teacher at Robert E. Lee High School (Tyler, Texas) worked together with the school's business and art departments to publish a 215-page guidebook, *Down Country Roads*, which offers essays, short stories, poems and illustrations of local historical sites. The project provided myriad learning opportunities: researching, interviewing, writing, decision-making, marketing, and so on. *Down Country Roads* is a quality book that has been in great demand throughout the community and the state.

These are just a few examples of quality work that we can see in schools when teachers understand the involve-me level of learning.

Figure 2

Experience and Learning

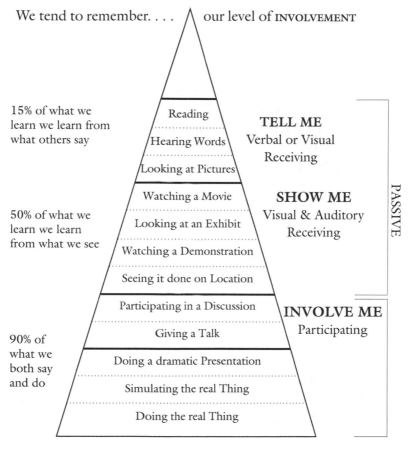

We tend to remember. . . . our level of INVOLVEMENT

15% of what we learn we learn from what others say

Reading
Hearing Words
Looking at Pictures

TELL ME
Verbal or Visual
Receiving

50% of what we learn we learn from what we see

Watching a Movie
Looking at an Exhibit
Watching a Demonstration
Seeing it done on Location

SHOW ME
Visual & Auditory
Receiving

PASSIVE

90% of what we both say and do

Participating in a Discussion
Giving a Talk
Doing a dramatic Presentation
Simulating the real Thing
Doing the real Thing

INVOLVE ME
Participating

Cone of Learning

Figure 3

Bloom's Taxonomy and the Quality School

I. **KNOWLEDGE**=Recognition of Information
    1. Define   4. Label   7. Narrate
    2. List   5. Record   8. Recall
    3. Memorize   6. Repeat   9. Report

II. **COMPREHENSION**=Understanding Information
    1. Describe   4. Report   7. Recognize
    2. Explain   5. Review   8. Discuss
    3. Identify   6. Express   9. Locate

III. **APPLICATION**=Applying Knowledge to Solve Problems
    1. Demonstrate   4. Illustrate   7. Interpret
    2. Practice   5. Operate   8. Interview
    3. Apply   6. Translate   9. Dramatize

IV. **ANALYSIS**= Separating Information as it Applies to Various Situations
    1. Distinguish   4. Solve   7. Experiment
    2. Compare   5. Question   8. Debate
    3. Inventory   6. Diagram   9. Differentiate

V. **EVALUATION**=Judgements as to Usefulness
    1. Select   4. Assess   7. Value
    2. Judge   5. Rate   8. Measure
    3. Predict   6. Prioritize   9. Choose

VI. **SYNTHESIS**=Applying Information to Improve Quality of Situation and Life
    1. Propose   4. Design   7. Prepare
    2. Arrange   5. Compose   8. Assemble
    3. Organize   6. Classify   9. Formulate

Chapter 3

From External Motivation
to Internal Motivation

We often treat the people whom we supervise as if we can force them to do what we want. Such thinking—that we can coerce people to do what we want them to do even if they do not want to do it—is consistent with stimulus-response theory which presupposes the efficacy of external motivation. Simply stated, stimulus-response theory maintains that rewards will increase the frequency of a behavior and punishments will decrease it. A proponent of the stimulus-response theory of motivation might analyze a behavior this way: the ringing of a telephone is the stimulus; your response is to pick up the handset and say hello. Essentially, this is saying that something outside you controls your behavior. If this were true, then every time the phone rings you would be compelled to answer it. But we all know that isn't true. Sometimes we do not want to talk with anyone, so we just let the phone ring. Or sometimes we are busy, so we let our answering machine take the message. A belief in external motivation is a belief that our behavior is determined by factors and events apart from ourselves. When we were students, this is how teachers usually treated us. This is how school administrators usually try to motivate teachers.

People who adopt this style have not learned that there is another way to motivate people by internal motivation, which is based on control theory. The only way we will be able to have quality schools and quality relationships—with cooperation between students and teachers, teachers and administrators, employers and employees—is to understand internal motivation and control theory, knowing that people are motivated from within, not from outside forces such as rewards and punishment. This key concept is perhaps the most important new paradigm to understand and apply in order to create quality organizations.

Control theory, as explained by Dr. William Glasser, states that all our behavior is based on five basic needs that are innate: survival, fun, freedom, love or belonging, and power (see Figure 4). All of our behavior is our best attempt to meet one or more of these needs. If we want students to learn to love reading, it will only happen when they see that reading is fun. It satisfies their needs for power and freedom when they have choices of what they can read.

In many of our schools we seem to be teaching students to hate reading. How can that be? We tell them what to read and assign reading that they do not see as meeting any of their needs. If they refuse to read, we punish them for not cooperating. We use textbooks which are intimidating for many students. We assign large quantities of reading instead of focusing on quality. This dilemma is explained thoroughly in Mary Leonhardt's excellent book, *Parents Who Love Reading, Kids Who Don't* (1993).

When we focus on how good it feels to read something that is enjoyable, it can satisfy our needs for power, fun, and freedom. This improves the quality of our lives and leads to true lifelong learning. When educators design curriculum that focuses on quality as opposed to quantity, so that students see learning as being useful now and in the future because it meets one or more of their basic needs, then we will see students doing the quality work that they are capable of, the quality work which we see so infrequently in our schools today.

The old stimulus-response, external approach to motivation will seem to work in a teacher-student relationship under two conditions: the student is dependent on the reward, or he is afraid of the punishment. Relationships based on fear and dependence, however, cannot be sustained. Fear and dependency destroy quality. If students do not want smiling faces, stars, points, goodies, and other types of rewards, they will resist doing the work. If they are not afraid of staying after school, going to the principal's office, being suspended, having parents contacted, losing points, or receiving a sad face, they will not cooperate. Many teachers are frustrated in today's classrooms because students are becoming less dependent on our rewards and less fearful of our punishments. External ways of coercing them to do what we want are becoming ineffective.

We set ourselves up for failure in using rewards and punishment by saying to students, "Do this and I'll give you that." Do this paper and I will give you points, stars, credit, smiling face, a good grade, etc. Whenever we add the *that* onto the *this*, we devalue the *this*. Students think, "This must not be worth doing, in and of itself, because they need to bribe me with that to get me to do it." Students begin to view that as more important than this. Let's say a teacher tells her students that when they each read four books (this), she will give them a pizza party (that). That becomes more important than this, so the students read shorter, simpler books with big print and lots of pictures to get done faster, to get the pizza. They cannot answer questions about what they have read because they were focusing on the that, not on the this. In quality schools the this—reading—should be satisfying in and of itself, because it satisfies one's need for power, it is fun and enjoyable. It meets internal needs because of its usefulness.

The more often teachers use rewards, the more students seem to need them. They exchange something internally valuable for some type of external goody. But when the pizza is eaten, the goody is gone.

When we reward students to get them to do something, we are assuming they would not choose to do it on their own. We demean and devalue the learning process. Dozens of studies provide convincing evidence that people who are trying to earn a reward end up doing a poorer job on many tasks than people who are not rewarded for the same tasks. When we use bribes, we are presuming that students are basically lazy. We found that when we bribed Apollo students with rewards, they did exactly what was necessary to get the reward and no more. Rewards also set up competition instead of cooperation. Cooperation builds trust, opens communication, and increases a person's willingness to ask questions or ask for assistance. This is precisely what rewards and punishments destroy.

Can rewards work? Yes! But they only motivate people to get rewards, not to do quality work. If the goal is quality work, no artificial reward can match the power of meeting basic needs, taking knowledge, and seeing how that knowledge will add quality to our lives now and in the future. When students perceive that what a teacher is asking them to do is relevant and useful as well as satisfying, they continue to do their work on their own—during lunch break, staying after school, or even coming back at night. Learning centers at Apollo High School were open two nights a week for students who wanted to have more time to complete their work. Sierra Mountain High School (Grass Valley, California) is open four evenings a week from 3-8 p.m. for students who want to do more work, make up work, or improve the quality of some work that they are not satisfied with. This is evidence of true, self-directed, lifelong learning.

Mark Lepper, in his book *The Hidden Cost of Reward* (1978), reported that a student's interest typically declines when he is working for a reward, compared to doing work that is worthwhile in and of itself. Dr. W. Edwards Deming, in his book *The New Economics for Industry, Government, Education* (1993), says that application of external motivation (rewards and punishment) is "the most powerful inhibitor to quality and productivity in the western world. It builds fear, nourishes short-term performance, annihilates long-term planning, demolishes teamwork, nourishes rivalry and leaves people bitter."

When we create a sense of involvement and ownership, which creates the commitment that generates the pride, then and only then will we see students doing quality work which becomes a need-satisfying experience in learning. Let me share some specific examples of how quality work arises from students meeting their basic needs—from the application of control-theory principles of internal motivation.

After reading about damage done in California by the January 1994 earthquake, students in a social studies class at a middle school in Texas felt they wanted to do something to help. The class devised four ways to raise funds to help one particular school in Ventura County that they had read about, and working together they raised more than $2,000. In a letter to the damaged school, they explained how they had raised this money to help replace classroom materials lost in the earthquake. Although they have never met, students from both schools have continued to write back and forth. No extrinsic rewards were needed to motivate the Texas students—the internal need to reach out and help others (love/belonging) initiated the project, and the way the teacher allowed them to plan and carry out the project satisfied their internal needs for freedom, power, and fun.

At Apollo High School, a group of students complained to me that they did not like the blacktop area between our biological and physical science buildings. I asked them how they could make it look better. By asking what they wanted to do about it and then letting them go ahead with their idea, their need for freedom was considered. They agreed it would be much nicer to have a garden, and they figured out how they could make one. Working together to create a garden between the two buildings, helping and cooperating with each other, satisfied their need for love and belonging.

Their need for power was met with the recognition they received. Staff and other students told them over and over how beautiful the area looked, what a great job they had done. And even though it was hard work, they had a lot of fun designing and working at something different, something out of the ordinary. Furthermore, their sense of ownership and pride created a willingness to maintain the garden, and they continuously generated new ideas for improving it. Meeting their basic needs was more than adequate motivation. No one had to bribe them to get the job done.

Similarly, when a group of girls complained that their restroom looked bad, I asked them, "What would you like to do about it?" Working together, they completely cleaned and redecorated the restroom—from putting down new floor tiles to painting murals on the walls. Working together on this project met all of their needs for fun, power, freedom, and love and belonging. They were proud of their work and maintained the pleasant appearance they had created.

For a deeper understanding of control theory and internal motivation, I recommend reading Dr. Glasser's books, *Control Theory Manager* (1994) and *Control Theory in the Classroom* (1986); Perry Good's book, *In Pursuit of Happiness* (1987), which in a very creative way describes the basic needs; and Barnes Boffey's book, *Reinventing Yourself* (1993), especially the chapter on total behavior. Understanding control theory is the foundation to building quality relationships in our schools and eliminating fear and dependency by meeting students' basic needs. The feeling of pride and accomplishment lasts as long as one thinks about the quality work that was created, as compared to a pizza which only lasts until it is eaten. Using control theory eliminates the "Do this and you'll get that" syndrome which becomes a real barrier to doing quality work in most of our schools.

Figure 4
Basic Needs
1. **Survival**
   A) Food   C) Shelter
   B) Clothing   D) Safety
2. **Love and Belonging**
   A) Giving and Receiving Love
   B) Support and Friendship
   C) Involvement and Connectedness
   D) Acceptance and Appreciation
3. **Power**
   A) Skills and Achievement
   B) Competence and Influence
   C) Recognition by Ourselves and Others
   D) Continuous Improvement
4. **Freedom**
   A) To Act and Think without Restriction
   B) Choices and Independence
   C) Acting on Own without Coercion
   D) Autonomy and Liberty
5. **Fun**
   A) Pleasure and Enjoyment
   B) Learning and Laughter
   C) Play and Recreation

Chapter 4

From the Outside In
to the Inside Out

Another way to understand control theory is to understand the paradigm shift from operating our lives from the outside in to the inside out. As the Apollo students were learning control theory (living from the inside out) and giving up stimulus-response theory (living from the outside in), the following was one of the most effective strategies that helped them understand and internalize their understanding.

We drew a diagram on the chalkboard like the one below. Inside a circle we put "you." Your feelings, thoughts, attitudes, decisions, actions, success, and personality are all inside the circle. Outside the circle are your friends, parents, teachers, money, gangs, part-time job, school work, activities, situations, drugs and alcohol, and the weather.

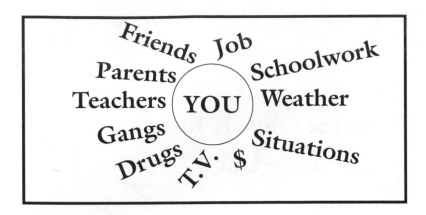

We then asked the students nine key questions:

1. Where is the responsibility for your attitudes?
2. Where is the responsibility for your actions and your behavior?
3. Where is the responsibility for your feelings?
4. Where is the responsibility for whether you learn in school or not?
5. Where is the responsibility for all these things? Is it inside your circle or outside your circle?
6. Do others cause you to use drugs or alcohol, or is it a choice you make?
7. Can others force you to work part-time to earn some money, or is that your choice?
8. Do others cause you to feel angry or hurt, or is that something you have control over? Is how you feel something you choose, or is it something that others control?
9. If someone calls you a "low-life loser" does that mean it is true, or do you choose to believe it is true?

The Apollo students, as well as most other students we have worked with at both elementary and secondary levels, answered that the responsibility for these things is inside their circle. Other people cannot make them upset or make them feel inferior without their consent.

Then we asked the students, "Have you ever been at the beach, in a park, or on an outing, and it began to rain?" We asked those who said yes, "What happened to your day at the beach or park when it began to rain?" Their replies tended to be similar: "The rain ruined the day!" "The rain really sucks when you are at the beach." "It's the rain's fault that the day was ruined." "I cursed the rain for destroying our day at the beach." We then asked them, "While you were blaming and cursing the rain, was it possible that a block away someone else was blessing the rain?" When they agreed that was possible, we asked them, "How could someone curse the rain and someone else bless the rain? Rain is rain—how could the same rain cause one person to be unhappy and, at the same time, another to be happy?"

We asked the students, "Was rain something inside your circle or outside your circle?" They all answered that it was outside their circle. As we took each item listed outside their circle, we went through this same process and we discovered that even though they said their feelings and attitudes were their responsibility, thus inside their circle, most of them blamed all the things outside their circle for how they felt, for their attitude, and for their happiness.

The last thing we asked the students was, "Did any of you have a lousy day this week?" Several students answered yes and described why they had a lousy day. Reasons for the lousy day included: my parents never listen, that teacher is unfair, sometimes my friends let me down, things just were not going well for me, some people have all the luck but me, I got caught taking drugs last week and got in trouble. All these things were outside their circle. Then we asked if anyone in the class had a terrific day while these other students were having a lousy day. Many answered yes and described why they had a good day. We talked about why some people had a great day, while others had a lousy day. What makes a day good? The things outside our circle or our attitude towards those things outside our circle? Where is your attitude? Inside or outside your circle? Of course, "Inside my circle" was their reply. What can we control? Those things outside our circle or our attitude towards those things outside our circle?

They began to realize that we can only control our own attitudes. Happiness is not in having things, but enjoying the things we have. They began to understand that happiness is not in finding the right person but in being the right person. They began to see that it was a waste of their time and energy to blame all the things outside their circle for how they felt and that it would be much more effective to spend that time and energy living from the inside out.

They began to understand that stimulus-response is living from the outside in, and control theory is living from the inside out. Living from the inside out increases one's sense of power and helps to meet the other basic needs of fun, freedom, love and belonging. They become more responsible and have more control when they live from the inside out. Living from the outside in was giving up their responsibility or control to all those things outside their circle. It was letting other people, things, and the weather determine and be in control of their feelings. They wanted to be in charge of their own lives by living from the inside out.

We discussed the following key approaches to how to live from the inside out:

1. I only allow into my circle what I believe. If I believe no one can make me feel inferior without my consent, then I am responsible for my own life.
2. The difference is not what is, the difference is my attitude towards it and how I let it affect me, whether I let it in my circle or not.
3. Living from the outside in is not much fun because I am allowing others to control and determine my day, my feelings, and the direction my life is going is in their hands. As Wayne Dyer put it in his book, *Pulling Your Own Strings* (1977), I am letting others pull my strings, and since I gave them to others, I can take them back and pull my own strings, from the inside out.
4. The choice is mine. I can spend my life reacting to and blaming what is outside my circle for how I feel and continue to say I am not responsible, I am powerless. Or I can take responsibility for my life, and if there are problems I can work to improve them instead of blaming and being immobilized by them.

5. If someone calls me a name, it is only an opinion, and if it is not true, I do not have to act like it is.

6. Others only reflect to me what I already believe about myself, what is inside my circle.

7. Others are not responsible for my happiness, nor am I responsible for theirs. Happiness is something that comes from within as I live my life by my values and principles.

8. Others who tap into my circle will get out of it what I allow in. If I have love and understanding for myself, inside my circle, then I will show others care and understanding.

9. The maximum performer operates out of love, not fear.

10. I can choose to be "reactive," to live from the outside in, but it is better if I choose to be "proactive," to live from the inside out.

11. Stress is caused by what goes on between my ears, from the inside out, not by anything outside my circle.

12. Self-evaluation becomes very important in living from the inside out. When I begin to feel uncomfortable, I want to ask myself, "Am I living from the outside in or from the inside out? What can I do to make this situation better?"

13. When I forgive myself and others and try to learn from my mistakes, I can improve the quality of my life. When I blame others, I move nowhere, I make no progress.

14. My security comes from living by my values and beliefs. When I treat others the way I want to be treated, I increase my chances that others will treat me that way too!

As people learn control theory and adopt the perspective of living from the inside out, they also accept responsibility for their feelings and behavior. At Dent Middle School (South Carolina), a physical-education teacher made a point of having his students learn control theory. Working in groups of three, the students became involved in problem-solving through class discussions. In a period of one month, classroom disruptions decreased by eighty percent, from thirty-one interruptions the first week to only seven during the fourth week. The time initially spent learning control theory was more than paid back by fewer disruptions during the rest of the term, which meant more time for active participation.

Even difficult students can learn control theory concepts, to everyone's benefit. A special-education teacher at Newman Smith High School (Carrollton, Texas) demonstrated considerable success with her class of fourteen- to eighteen-year-old learning-disabled and emotionally disturbed students. Her students not only created their own rules, but their own discipline procedures as well. In essence, she empowered them to be part of the solution instead of just punishing them for bad behavior. She also gave them more responsibility for their own learning and encouraged them to evaluate their own work and make improvements. To test how well her approach was working, she got permission from her principal to come to class thirty minutes late one day. When she arrived, she found all of her students working on task, being responsible. Most just smiled at her and continued on with their work. On several other occasions when she arrived late, the results were the same.

Faculty dynamics also change as teachers shift their thinking from stimulus-response to control theory. It energizes them to make changes, whereas previously they may have engaged in chronic complaining or quiet subversion. When the teachers at Robert E. Lee High School (Tyler, Texas) saw the need to rewrite their curriculum and to develop instructional strategies such as team teaching, interdisciplinary studies, and integrated approaches to make learning more meaningful, they decided to have a longer school day so there would be time for an extra conference period to work together. This teacher-driven initiative resulted in a new flexible schedule which gave them time to accomplish their curriculum-writing tasks while also giving students an additional period to pursue an area of interest.

Chapter 5

From Individual Work and Competition to Teamwork and Cooperation

There are basically three ways of achieving one's goals: competitively, which means working against others; independently, which means working without regard for others; and cooperatively, which means working with others. Independent work and competition dominated at least seventy-five percent of the teaching methods at Apollo High School before we began the process of becoming a quality school. Most of the students worked individually, competing with others for the best grades.

Competition creates winners and losers. It dampens creativity, causes stress, and fosters distrust and deceit. In schools it impairs learning and performance. Students focus more on winning than on learning or on doing quality work. Competition gives rise to cheating and winning at any expense. Students who see they cannot win become discouraged. Competitive people constantly measure themselves against others even in situations which do not call for it. [For more on the negative aspects of competition, see Alfie Kohn's book, *No Contest: The Case Against Competition* (1987).]

Competing simply means that one is working toward a goal in such a way as to prevent others from reaching their goals. But success in achieving a goal does not necessarily require winning over others, just as failing to achieve a goal does not necessarily mean losing to others. Human beings strive for goals, but striving with others (cooperation) or against others (competition) are learned behaviors. A school's learning activities, evaluation methods and approaches to solving problems all reflect whether it is teaching competition or cooperation.

A quality school de-emphasizes individual work and competition and focuses instead on building teamwork and cooperation. As mentioned in Chapter 2, teamwork and cooperation are two of the most important skills that personnel directors are looking for in prospective employees. As seen by business managers, the key competencies essential for success in the 21st-century workplace are an individual's ability to participate as a member of a team, to teach others new skills, to negotiate, and to work well with men and women from diverse backgrounds. More books are being written now about teamwork and cooperative learning than ever before. Research shows us that cooperation is most conducive to quality work. Quality schools make teamwork a regular experience, because learning the skills for working in groups is crucial for the students' future success.

Getting students to work individually is usually easier than getting them to work productively in groups, but there are important advantages to working in groups. Working in groups increases opportunities for students to meet their basic needs, compared to when they work alone.

The need for belonging, especially, is better met in groups, but group work also can satisfy the needs for recognition and fun. When independent work means sitting silently in one's seat, group work also provides more freedom. Work is more likely to be of high quality when it satisfies one's basic needs. David Johnson and colleagues, in *Circles of Learning* (1984), show that people who feel accepted by others feel safe enough to explore problems more freely, take risks, play with possibilities, and benefit from self-evaluation of mistakes rather than endure a climate in which mistakes must be hidden to avoid ridicule (the results of a competitive environment). Teamwork is focused on doing one's best without any interest in being better than others.

Several creative minds are bound to be better than one. There will be more ideas to start with, and they lead to other ideas, so the results are much richer than if everyone worked individually. The quality of solutions and work increases significantly when students work as a team. A good definition for TEAM is "Together Everyone Achieves More."

If a group comprises students with complementary skills and compensating strengths, the group's ability to accomplish a task will surpass the ability of any one of its members, even the most talented. The simplest form of teamwork or cooperation is one student helping another. At the Westinghouse Vocational Technology School (Brooklyn, New York), students are paired to help, tutor and support each other. Also, seniors serve as mentors to freshmen. After instituting these programs of students helping students, the school's dropout rate went from eighteen percent to less than seven percent, and the number of students who failed all their classes went from 227 the first year to only 11 the second year.

A variety of classroom projects can be devised that benefit from teamwork and cooperation for both their creation and their execution. At Bear River High School (Grass Valley, California), social studies teachers designate a topic, such as the Renaissance, along with key areas to be studied, such as art, history, science, English, and performing arts. In small groups, students brainstorm ideas for projects to reflect all these areas. The student groups then select one project to do in each area that will demonstrate their understanding of the Renaissance. For science they might build and explain how to use a catapult. For the English and performing-arts areas they could write and perform a short play which describes that period in history. The possibilities are enormous. Enthusiasm for these self-generated projects is high, as is the quality of the projects that are undertaken.

With careful planning and sufficient vision, some cooperative projects exceed even the teachers' expectations. A team of third-grade teachers at E. L. Kent Elementary School (Carrollton, Texas) developed an idea to provide their students with a quality experience for learning writing skills, accounting, math and speaking skills, along with advertising and video production, economics and history, planning and self-evaluations. During the school year the students created the "Blue Bonnet Café" in partnership with parents and business groups. The students wrote job descriptions for the café, applied for those positions on a rotating basis, completely ran the café from ordering supplies to cooking, accounting, setting up a checking account at a local bank, and making a profit. They opened a savings account to start the next year with initial capital. Working with a local business, the students made a television commercial, learning video production skills as well as presentation skills. The students constantly evaluated what was working, what needed to be improved, and ways they could make those improvements. They held planning sessions and continuously improved the quality of service, food, and operations of the Blue Bonnet Café. Next year, new third graders will assume the operation of the café so they can benefit from this quality experience.

The most important knowledge needed to move successfully from individual work to teamwork is how to determine who will be in each group. A common practice is simply to have students number off, one to four (or whatever number of groups is wanted), then have the ones get together as a group, the twos as a group, etc. The results, however, are highly uneven and unpredictable, because this procedure has no logic to it. It ignores students' learning styles, temperaments, and compatibility. Some groups work well together, and some do not.

The answer to this problem at Apollo High School was to first identify the students' learning styles. Teams comprised students of each learning style instead of having all the same learning style in one group. Each learning style has particular strengths, and by combining them, we increased the quality that each team produced. At Apollo the students who built playhouses for the elementary schools were placed in teams of five students with at least one of each learning style on a team. One team was in charge of the foundation, another the walls, another the roof, another the interior design, and the last the exterior design. All worked together, using the strength of each learning style, to create a quality project, the playhouse.

Identifying learning styles for all the students in a class is a challenge, but help is available. At Apollo High School we used a program called "True Colors." Based on the Myers-Briggs learning style assessment tool, combined with Kersay's temperament styles test, this program identifies four basic learning styles, which are represented by different colors. Students are given cards that describe the four styles and go through a five-step process to identify their strongest color, shaded by their next color and concluding with their pale color. Another tool for identifying learning styles is the PETALS program. PETALS also identifies four basic learning styles represented by colors. High school students discover their preferred learning style by completing and scoring a fifteen-item questionnaire. Other questionnaires target earlier grades, and parents or teachers complete the questionnaires for very young students. Identifying learning styles not only facilitates the assignment of students to cooperative groups, it also enables teachers to modify their teaching strategies as needed. Quality teachers know that if students are not learning the way you teach, you have to teach the way that they learn.

When teachers evaluate a student's work on the basis of how it compares to the work of other students, the teacher fosters competition rather than cooperation. One of the most harmful approaches used by many teachers is grading on a curve. With this process, a few students get A's or F's and the majority receive a B, C, or D. No get A's or F's and the majority receive a B, C, or D. No matter how well, overall, a class of students performs, the few with the highest scores get A's and some fail. Work that is graded on a curve is judged in comparison to the work of other students, not in comparison to a standard of excellence. Grading on a curve compels competition. The only way to get a high grade is to "beat" almost everyone else. In a quality school no one grades on a curve. "Quality" is the only standard against which a student's work is judged. If all students do quality work, all students earn high marks.

Some schools, most often in the early elementary grades, do not evaluate students by letter grades, but provide relatively extensive commentaries about the child's strengths, weaknesses, and progress in various areas. Or, as teachers at the Kate Sullivan School (Tallahassee, Florida) have done, they replace report cards with portfolios that contain examples of the student's work which student and teacher agree best demonstrate the quality of the work they can do.

A physical science teacher in Edina, Minnesota, discussed "What do grades mean?" with his students, and as a result, they decided to go on a pass/no pass system. The teacher developed a concurrent self-evaluation form on which the students described what they had done, what they had learned, how much time and effort they had put into it, what they felt good about, and how they might improve. Next, the teacher added comments and perceptions. The final step was for the students to explain the process and share the evaluations with their parents, who then added their comments. This process has eliminated much competition among students and encouraged more cooperation. It was so well received that other of the 130 students in the physical science classes, only ten parents still insisted on a letter grade.

Another advantage of teamwork and cooperation is that the chances of identifying and treating the causes of problems are greatly enhanced by working in groups, and the motivation to carry out those solutions is much greater. The quality of solutions for problems is at a much higher level when groups work together to find solutions.

To solve problems, the staff at Apollo High School would hold a short staff meeting to describe the problem, then break into teams of seven teachers, including at least one of each learning style, which would meet in any place on campus of their choosing for the next forty-five minutes. All the teams then returned to share their solutions with the other groups. This process created better solutions, greater involvement, and improved cooperation. With adoption of the team process, the staff's rating of the effectiveness of faculty meetings went from 5.0 to 8.5 on a scale of 1 to 10 (10 being excellent).

The cooperative effort of students and teachers at Brady Elementary School (Chesaning, Michigan) solved a long-standing problem with lunch-hour discipline and behavior during recess. Instead of making more rules or increasing the severity of punishments, the group decided to completely restructure the lunch hour. Originally, all 240 children ate lunch in the gym then went outside for free play. With the new plan, students eat their lunch in the classroom with their teachers. Then for thirty minutes they participate in "Choice Time." Early in the day, students sign up for one of the offered activities, such as volleyball, clay, reading, board games, computers, Legos, etc., which are supervised by support staff, monitors and parents. Everyone enjoys eating in the classrooms because it is quieter and allows teachers to talk with students on a personal basis. During Choice Time, students are learning and improving social skills while teachers are free to have some time together.

Chapter 6

From Boss Management
to Lead Management

In a quality school, administrators and teachers must act as managers. They need to persuade the students that working hard, producing quality work, and following their teachers' agenda will ultimately add quality to their own lives as well as to the lives of others. But administrators and teachers must understand the important distinctions between being "boss" managers and "lead" managers. Quality schools have lead managers.

A boss manager acts as referee, cop, and dictator. A boss manager uses coercion and relies on rewards and punishment (external motivation) to try to get people to do what the boss wants. A lead manager, on the other hand, acts as facilitator, coach, enthusiast, cheerleader, and nurturer of quality. A lead manager helps people to meet their basic needs (internal motivation), because the lead manager knows that true motivation comes from within a person. A lead manager works to identify causes, then treats the causes so the behavior problems disappear. In a school, administrators and teachers all act as lead managers. Administrators will be trying to lead teachers toward quality while the teachers, in turn, will be trying to lead their students toward quality. Students, too, benefit from learning lead management skills. The Oak Meadow School (San Antonio, TX) developed an entire student leadership curriculum for fifth and sixth graders, including an impressive training manual, based on principles of lead management described in Stephen R. Covey's *The Seven Habits of Highly Effective People* (1989).

The chart in Figure 5 contrasts many characteristics of boss managers and lead managers, but there are still other important characteristics of lead managers to consider. Lead managers listen well and accept other people's ideas. They communicate effectively, persuading others to share their vision. They are enthusiastic, energetic, dependable, and structured, yet flexible. While being goal-oriented, they anticipate consequences. They approach life positively. They tackle problems and face challenges willingly. They develop themselves to their highest potential.

Lead managers treat everyone with respect and dignity. They set an example for others to follow. They make themselves available and visible to others. They show confidence in all of their coworkers. Lead managers remain loyal to their followers and to their common vision. They build group cohesiveness and pride. Only when leaders create a sense of involvement and ownership do they create the commitment and pride in people that lead them to produce the highest quality work of which they are capable.

Lead managers realize that problems are almost always the fault of the system, not the people, so they spend their time and energy identifying causes. When confronted with a problem, they don't ask, "Who is to blame?" Instead they ask, "What is the problem, and how can we solve it?" They empower students and teachers to become a part of the solution, rather than blaming them for being part of the problem. They insist on quality, holding everyone accountable, including themselves. They establish effective evaluation procedures which include both concurrent and self-evaluation techniques. They maintain a strong awareness of continuous improvement. They are active coaches. Lead managers see people as their greatest resource and spend much of their time and energy working with people, as compared to boss managers, who spend a lot of time working with things.

Research over the past thirty years has validated the benefits of lead management techniques in industry and education. When management and workers share in the decision-making process, respect and trust one another, and establish a healthy interpersonal communication process, morale, productivity, and job satisfaction increase. Mutual problem-solving takes time, but its effectiveness makes the endeavor genuinely worthwhile. Let me share with you several examples of what can happen as schools change from boss management to lead management.

Originally, I tended to be a boss manager. For instance, any time students were found to be under the influence of drugs or alcohol, I would immediately suspend them, possibly even expel them. This means I was treating the symptom, not the cause. When I asked students what they did while they were suspended, most said that they went someplace unsupervised and used more drugs, because they felt bad about having been caught. They felt that someone who they thought cared about them (me) obviously did not care. But punishing people does not lead to more effective behaviors. It builds barriers and creates distance. Punishment does not create the quality relationships that we want in a quality school.

Once I had learned the principles of lead management, we developed a new approach at Apollo High School to deal with students who exhibited drug and alcohol problems. The Student Assistance Program, as it was called, created a support group so students could meet regularly with others who had similar problems. Our Student Assistance Program was similar to the twelve-step AA program which has been one of the most successful and lasting programs anywhere for people with addiction problems. Each student was assigned a buddy from the group. The student could call the buddy if he or she wanted help sorting out their feelings, to avoid the destructive choice of addiction. Outside guests were invited to speak with the group about how they overcame their drug or alcohol problem and to answer students' questions. The group, under the guidance of a teacher, was able to discuss issues openly and honestly because trust and mutual respect were built among the members. Students began to see that they had the power to choose to use drugs or alcohol or to make a more responsible choice—to seek help to deal effectively with any conflicts they were facing. The Student Assistance Program proved to be a much different and more effective approach than punishing students, which usually just made the problems worse.

As a "boss," I would simply tell students who had misbehaved, "This is the rule. You have broken the rule. This is the punishment." If they had been fighting, for instance, I suspended them for three days. I did not listen to any reasons why they got into the fight. As a boss manager often does, I pointed to the punished students as an example to others—if you behave this way, this is what we will do to you, too. Obviously, what I was doing was not working, because we continued to have several fights each month. When I learned how to be a lead manager, I began listening to the students. I moved from treating symptoms to looking for causes, the reasons why students got to the point where they found it necessary to fight. Once the causes were identified and dealt with, the behavior problem disappeared. During my entire last year at Apollo High School, only a single fight took place.

Before being introduced to the principles of lead management, playground supervisors at the Colbert School (Mead, Washington) had been sending forty to fifty students a week to detention for unacceptable behavior and rules violations. After learning lead management strategies, they decided to replace the detention room with a "planning room" where students would discuss rules, behaviors, consequences, and how to change their behavior. To return to the playground, the students had to devise a plan that would help them behave more responsibly. Within eight weeks of instituting the planning room, disruptions on the playground and in the hallways had dwindled to only five or six a week.

During my former life as a boss manager, I wrote a mission statement for our school, but my mission never really became the school's mission. The teachers did little more than was necessary to show me they were somewhat supportive. I could tell they were not truly committed. Once I had learned how to be a lead manager, I quit trying to rally the teachers around "my cause." Instead, I involved them in creating a new mission statement for Apollo High School. The teachers and I sat down together, in many meetings for many hours, to discuss what our students should be like when they graduated from Apollo. What skills should they be able to demonstrate? We covered three walls of a classroom with paper. One at a time, each teacher went up with a marker and listed the skills he or she thought our students should be able to demonstrate once they graduated. When the last teacher had finished, more than 150 skills were listed! Then I gave each teacher twenty peel-off colored dots and asked them to walk around, read each of the statements written on the walls, and to evaluate them. I directed them to stick a dot beside the twenty skills that they thought were most important. By the end, twenty-eight skills stood out clearly. Then we sat down together to write a mission statement that incorporated the aims we had decided on as a group. This mission statement turned out to be one that the entire staff was committed to, and the staff worked hard to make it a reality. Teachers are much more motivated to find success in a mission statement they have helped to create, as opposed to one imposed on them from above.

Developing a mission statement and shared vision at Kate Sullivan School (Tallahassee, Florida) involved not only teachers and the principal, but PTA members, support staff, and district and university personnel as well. In so doing, they established five "core values" which guided their efforts:

1. Individuals are valued.
2. Teachers are professional educators.
3. Parents are partners.
4. Decision-making is shared.
5. Teachers are team members.

Values four and five were crucial for creating involvement and commitment to quality. One result of this process was that staff stopped asking, "What should we teach?" and began asking, "What is worth learning?" Focus changed from the teachers' needs to the students' needs as they became "managers" as much as teachers.

When I was still a boss manager, the only evaluation that concerned me was the one that the assistant superintendent completed on my performance every other year. But I began to realize that the assistant superintendent was rarely at our school, so he had few experiences on which to base his evaluation. As I became a lead manager, I started to question how accurate the assistant superintendent's evaluation could be. I began wondering if my own perceptions of the job that I was doing matched the perceptions of my staff. They were undoubtedly more knowledgeable about the job I was doing than the assistant superintendent! I made up an evaluation form on which the teachers, anonymously, could give me feedback. When there were discrepancies in our perceptions, I recognized what I needed to work on so that the teachers would perceive me more as a lead manager than a boss manager. When our perceptions agreed, it confirmed that I was doing something right and should continue with it.

In the Kenmore School District (New York), the staff regularly surveys parents, seeking feedback to three questions:

1. Are you satisfied with the education your child is receiving in this district?
2. Is there anything you are unhappy about with the district?
3. Do you have any suggestions as to how we can improve the quality of our schools?

At regular meetings a Quality Steering Committee, composed of teachers, support staff, students, parents, community members and business people, considers input from the parent surveys, listens to one another's ideas on various issues, and recommends ways to improve the quality of the schools. This process guarantees that the system does not stagnate and that changes are likely to be successful because they are initiated with widespread support.

In summary, the more that our relationships can move from "power over," which is boss management, to "power with," which is lead management, the more effective teachers will be in their teaching and students will be in their learning. Lead managers are catalysts in the creation of quality schools.

Figure 5

A Boss Manager

1. Judges others
2. Blames people for problems
3. Says, "I am not as bad as a lot of other people"
4. Controls
5. Takes himself and others for granted
6. Covers up mistakes
7. Says, "I only work here."
8. Demands
9. Builds walls
10. Drives his people
11. Depends on authority
12. Inspires fear
13. Says "I"
14. Gets there on time
15. Fixes blame for the breakdown
16. Knows how it is done
17. Says "Go."
18. Uses people
19. Sees today

20. Commands
21. Never has enough time

22. Is concerned with things
23. Treats the symptoms
24. Lets his people know where he stands
25. Does things right
26. Works hard to produce

27. Creates fear
28. Takes the credit
29. Seeks first to be understood
30. Has a win-lose approach to conflict resolution.

A Lead Manager

1. Accepts others
2. Looks for solutions
3. Says, "I am good but not as good as I can be."
4. Leads
5. Appreciates himself and others

6. Admits mistakes
7. Does more than his job
8. Asks
9. Builds communication
10. Coaches his people
11. Depends on cooperation
12. Inspires enthusiasm
13. Says "We"
14. Gets there ahead of time
15. Fixes the breakdown
16. Shows how it is done
17. Says, "Let's go."
18. Develops people
19. Looks at today as well as the future
20. Models
21. Makes time for things that count

22. Is concerned with people
23. Identifies and treats the causes
24. Lets his people know where they stand
25. Does the right thing
26. Works hard to get his people to produce
27. Creates confidence in others
28. Gives the credit to others
29. Seeks first to understand
30. Has a win-win approach to solving problems

Chapter 7

From Fear to Trust

In *Driving Fear Out of the Workplace* (1991), Kathleen Ryan talks about the different fears common to many organizations. Among them are the fear of speaking up or sharing ideas because we might be ridiculed or put down, the fear of participating because we might be criticized, and the fear of taking risks and being creative because we might fail. Certainly, the same fears flourish in schools as well. A particularly damaging fear is that of failure. Thomas Edison is supposed to have said, "I've never failed. I've just found out many ways that things don't work." Educators, especially, should keep Edison's perspective in mind.

Fear can be reduced by eliminating coercion, as discussed in the last chapter, and by building trust. Creating a quality environment, where people can do their best, requires building trust. Trust brings out the best in people. In quality schools, where trust is high, teachers and parents willingly express their thoughts, feelings, opinions, and concerns. This information enhances their ability to deal with problems. Participants in effective negotiations listen attentively and respectfully. They focus on issues, not on personalities nor positions. They seek solutions instead of scapegoats. When trust is low, turnover among staff members will be frequent, and those who do remain develop an attitude of "It's good enough," rather than an attitude of continuous improvement.

In my workshops on creating quality schools, I emphasize the five C's that build trust: Communication, Cooperation, Commitment, Concern, and Caring. Trust is built only with effort, time, and patience, but it can be easily and quickly destroyed. The four C's that destroy trust are Criticism, Comparison, Complaining, and Competition.

In his book, *The Seven Habits of Highly Effective People* (1990), Stephen R. Covey states that trust is built when we seek first to understand, then to be understood. Listening leads to understanding, thus providing a foundation for cooperation and growth in interpersonal relationships. When we listen effectively to what others have to say, chances are improved that we will be listened to in return.

To build trust we must let others know what we value, what we hope for, and what we want. Self-disclosure builds trust, as does admitting mistakes. Many people never admit mistakes for fear of losing their power or influence. They consider admitting mistakes to be a weakness. Experience shows, however, that letting others know one is human enhances a person's credibility. A leader builds trust, and reduces fear, when he or she allows people who have made mistakes, or failed at a task, to "make things right." As Diane Gossen explains in her book, *Restitution* (1993), self-discipline in students is enhanced when school personnel deal with infractions by encouraging restitution instead of resorting to punishment.

Following through with our commitments builds trust. First, we must let people know what we are willing, or not willing, to do. Then, we must meet their expectations by following through with our commitments and keeping our promises. Responsibilities should be delegated, and people allowed to carry out those responsibilities. How necessary is it to check on and control others? We must believe that others have integrity for there to be a trusting relationship.

Trust in others is built on courtesy, kindness, honesty, and openness. Trust improves when teachers deal directly with problems, instead of sending students to the office. Plainfield Elementary School (Saginaw, Michigan) has a plan whereby the principal and other support staff will cover classrooms when the teacher needs time with a student, one-on-one, to work through a behavior problem. When teachers are specifically trained to use communication and counseling skills, as they have been at Wheatland High School (Wheatland, Wyoming) and Ingram Middle School (Ingram, Texas), they solve problems with students directly, by themselves, rather than referring the students elsewhere for discipline. This reduces the number of office referrals and suspensions, thus freeing up counselors and principals to concentrate on their other responsibilities. Sensitivity to other people's needs and interests, appreciation and respect for other people's viewpoints help to build trust. Trust is built when there is pride and celebration in the achievement of others. And if we demonstrate our acceptance of others, the chances are greater that they will accept us.

The choice to trust another person requires a special perception—that the other person has our best interest in mind. The perception is that the other person wants to help, not hurt or blame. Trust is destroyed when a person perceives criticism and rejection. Trust develops when people feel safe and secure, when their thoughts and ideas are not ridiculed. To build trust, one must be loyal to those who are absent. For example, when someone criticizes a person who is absent, those present may fear that they, too, will some day be the target of criticism. Talking behind people's backs destroys trust. Acceptance reduces anxiety and one's fears about being vulnerable. Accepting other people without criticizing or judging them is important in building trust. It begins by accepting oneself.

Trust is enhanced when people begin to evaluate themselves, rather than being evaluated by others. Strengthening others, helping them to feel capable and powerful, also builds trust. Focusing time and energy on helping others to do things right is much more productive and satisfying than pointing out when they are wrong. Looking for ways to make ideas work, rather than for reasons why they will not, creates motivation to take risks, which boosts our chances of experiencing quality.

Reminding people of their weaknesses or holding grudges for past actions does little to encourage quality relationships and quality work. Common grading systems, in particular, never forgive a failure. For instance, if a ninth-grader cannot see why algebra is useful, he may do poorly and fail the course. Later, perhaps the student decides he wants to go to college and realizes that algebra is required for entrance, so he takes algebra again, works hard, and earns an A. What will appear on his transcript? Most schools never remove a failure from the student's record, or at the very best, they average an F and an A, recording a C. In a quality school, however, the A would replace the F, because A represents the level that the student eventually achieved and best describes his mastery of algebra.

My experiences as a teacher, counselor, and school principal have taught me that fear and lack of trust lead to what I have identified as the "Six R's":

1. **Resentment.** When we hurt students by punishing them—by humiliating them in front of other students, or taking away some activity they enjoy, or assigning them after-school detention, thus causing them to be late for work—we create resentment in the students. And resentment creates either a desire to get even or withdrawal.

2. **Resistance.** Some students begin to fight us and resist our efforts to gain their cooperation through threats and punishment because their basic need for freedom is being threatened.

3. **Rebellion.** When we try to control the students by making them dependent on the rewards and afraid of the punishments, some students meet their need for power by rebelling and refusing to cooperate.

4. **Retreat.** Some students retreat or withdraw from us because they are afraid. This happens more often with elementary students than secondary, but teachers all across the nation tell me that they are seeing this fear less frequently now. More and more elementary students are choosing to fight instead of giving way to threats.

5. **Reluctance.** We see this behavior in students as they refuse to cooperate. They choose to dawdle or do nothing.

6. **Revenge.** Students vandalize our schools to get even. Students engage in more fights—getting even and getting back at those who hurt them.

Research shows that punishment, as a means of getting obedience, causes students to resist, rebel, disobey, and defy. They become disrespectful, insubordinate, angry and belligerent. They start lying and hiding the truth. They blame others and tattle. They boss and bully others. They band together in gangs, forming alliances against authority. Or they become fearful, shy, timid, reluctant to try new things, afraid to speak the truth. They may withdraw, fantasize, and daydream.

When we use rewards to create a dependent relationship, students become more intent on the rewards than in wanting to learn. They may cheat, needing to win at any expense, or apple-polish to gain favor. They may become submissive, conforming, and docile. They may seek constant reassurance and approval, feeling secure and worthwhile only when others tell them they are worthwhile. They may begin to feel guilty, depressed, hopeless. They may develop eating disorders or abuse drugs and alcohol to get rid of feelings they do not want or to get a feeling they do not have. They may get become silent, passive, sick, or even suicidal. These results are not what teachers want, nor are they the outcomes teachers expected when they began their careers.

What we must do if our schools are ever going to become quality schools is to replace the "Six R's" with the "Six L's," as represented in the diagram below:

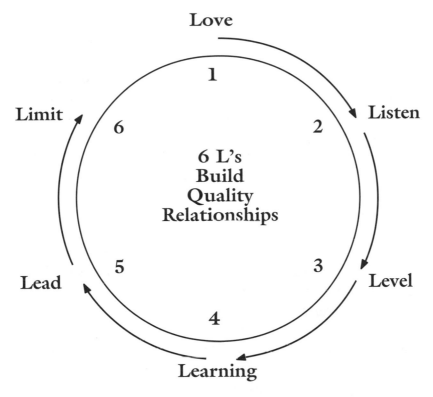

Love

1

Limit   Listen

6   2

6 L's
Build
Quality
Relationships

5   3

Lead   Level

4

Learning

The diagram of the Six L's is like a face of a clock, which symbolizes the time it takes to build a relationship and the importance of the sequence of L's.

1. **Love.** As a lead manager, I cannot simply demand respect by virtue of my position. I must earn it by the way I treat others. Relationships must be built on love, which helps to create the conditions for quality. Fear destroys it. We can tell students we love them a dozen times a day, but to be believed, we must show them.

2. **Listen.** We show our love when we listen to others without judging them. Listening not only shows we

NEW PARADIGMS FOR CREATING QUALITY SCHOOLS

care and accept others, but it helps us to identify real problems and to get to their causes, instead of just treating the symptoms. People usually tell those whom they trust how they feel. We need to hear about feelings and accept them, so we can move on to the behaviors and thoughts that are behind the feelings. Then, and only then, are we ready to resolve problems.

3. **Level.** The clock moves next to leveling, the skill of communicating about specific behavior, rather than attacking someone's character and personality. We cannot easily change our character and personality, so we become defensive when attacked. Leveling (also called reality therapy) is talking to students in a way that gets them to listen. It facilitates students wanting to be responsible by choosing more effective behaviors.

4. **Learning** in a quality school is a two-way street. Not only do students learn from teachers, but students and teachers learn from each other. Learning takes place beyond the school building, in the community and the home as well. Cooperation is emphasized and competition is minimized.

5. **Leading** is the fifth skill that builds quality. The best way to teach is by modeling—treating others in the way we want them to treat us. If we want respect, we must treat others with respect. If we want cooperation, we must cooperate also. We cannot tell someone how to be honest, how to do one's best, how not to give up, how to be a good sport. The only way that I know to teach or learn values is by example and observation.

6. **Limits.** The last skill is setting limits. There are rules in everything we do, and rules help to bring quality

to what we do. If you do not follow the rules to bake a cake, it may be inedible. Rules in games help us to enjoy the games. Rules in school help us to get along with each other. Rules and discipline (*not* punishment) are important in a quality school.

Now, the important thing for lead managers to realize is that they must run through the Six L's in proper sequence. Quality relationships are built on *love*, which is demonstrated by *listening* to others and helping them to take responsibility for their lives. A lead manager *levels* with people and encourages *learning* from each other. A lead manager *leads* by example and involves others to help set the *limits* that all can agree with and follow. In maintaining limits, the lead manager focuses on discipline and responsibility, not coercion and punishment.

For years, as an ineffective boss manager, I had the process reversed. I was running through the Six L's in counter-clockwise order: "These are the rules, my *limits*. I am here to *lead* you because I have credentials from the State of California. You are here because you have a lot to *learn*, so I will *level* with you and tell you what to learn, when to learn, and how to learn. Then I will test you, to see if you have learned it. I will reward you when you have and punish you when you have not. So you had better *listen* and do what I want you to do, when I want you to do it, and how I want you to do it. Then, if you do, I will probably *love* you and we will have a good year."

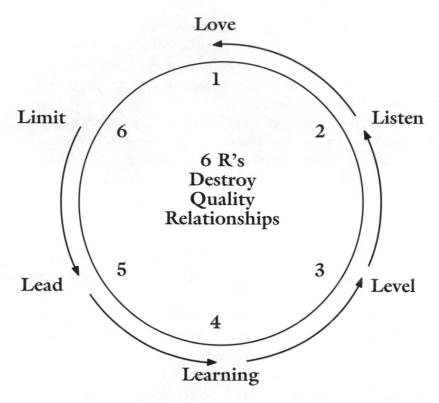

Doing the Six L's in reverse does *not* build quality relationships, but it does create the Six R's!

A person cannot become a leader in a quality school, or any organization, without learning how to build trust in others. Trust builds quality relationships, which precede the creation of a quality school environment, which enables students to do quality work.

Chapter 8

From Finding Fault
and Win-Lose Solutions
to Finding Win-Win Solutions

Boss managers assign blame and find fault with others for the problems they find in their schools. Typically, boss managers say that people in the schools—students, teachers, and parents—are the reasons there are problems. Lead managers, on the other hand, know that people within the system are rarely the problem—the system itself is the source of our problems. Boss managers try to make people do what they, the boss managers, want them to do. Lead managers work on the problems within the system and empower people within the system to be a part of the solution instead of blaming them for the problems.

Blaming leads to more blaming, never to finding solutions. When I work with high school teachers, they often blame the junior high teachers: "Why don't they keep students in the junior high school until they demonstrate they have the skills and maturity to enter high school?" When I work with junior high school teachers, they often blame the elementary teachers: "Why don't they keep children at the elementary level until they know how to read, write, and calculate?" When I work with elementary teachers, they often blame the parents: "I only have your children for five or six hours a day. If you don't reinforce their learning at home, I won't be able to do much." When I work with parents, they frequently blame the teachers for not doing the job they think they should be doing. Blaming leads to blaming which leads to more blaming.

My twenty-nine years of working in public school have taught me that we can only blame three things. We can blame ourselves, other people, or the establishment.

When we blame ourselves we are saying such things as: "I can never do anything right; it is my fault." As we blame ourselves we develop the mind-set that says "I'm not OK, but you are OK."

When we do not feel OK, we tend to put ourselves down and take all the blame, which creates guilt and depression. People who get depressed or—in control-theory terms—choose to depress, usually abuse themselves in some way. They make up a high percentage of the people who commit suicide, the second leading cause of death for teenagers in the United States. Many people abuse drugs and alcohol. Ask any adult or adolescent if a drug-induced feeling lasts or a drug-dampened feeling stays away, and they invariably answer no. Most realize that they have to keep taking more drugs.

The person who blames himself and puts himself down develops an attitude of "I should." I should or I shouldn't have done this or that, and because I didn't do what I should have done, I put myself down, find fault with myself, and I don't feel OK. These are the hallmarks of low self-esteem.

The second finger-pointing possibility is to blame others. When I blame another person, I put them down and find fault with them. My thinking is "I'm OK, but you are not OK."

When I see you as "not OK," I become angry, and if I cannot deal with my anger, then I become hostile. The damage I commit is not against myself but against others. I might fight you, stab you, shoot you. These are the kids we see that become gang members and try to meet their needs in irresponsible ways by hurting others. They develop the attitude "You should." You should have done this, or you shouldn't have done that, and so you are at fault—you're not OK, so you deserve what you get.

The final alternative is to blame the establishment. I can blame the parents, the teacher's union, the school board, the government, the students, or the school administration. When I blame the establishment, which of course I am a part of, I harbor the opinion "I'm not OK, but neither are you OK—all of us are screwed up!"

We become frustrated very easily when we blame the establishment. Any crime we commit is against the establishment. We might shoplift because we think "they" should lower prices or "they" should give us a raise so we can continue to buy things as prices increase. Because "they" do not give us what we want, we rip them off in some way. Teachers who blame the establishment may come to school unprepared to teach, or they race the students out of the parking lot at the end of the school day. The attitude we develop when we blame the establishment is "They should." And because they do not do what they should do, we get frustrated and do not give them our best.

So we blame ourselves, we blame others, or we blame the establishment. These are all examples of stimulus-response thinking. We are saying that things outside us control our behavior. Until we understand control theory and realize that others do not upset us—rather we choose to upset ourselves over what others do or fail to do—we will never make progress towards finding solutions to the many problems we face in our schools today. A student came up with this thought: "When we use control theory in our lives, we will not SHOULD on ourselves."

Dr. Haim Ginott, in his book *Teacher and Child* (1972), advises us never to blame, but to ask, "What is the problem and what are some solutions?" As we become lead managers, we create involvement and ownership in others by empowering them to be a part of the solution. We look at how we can improve the system to meet people's needs so they can work, be creative and do the kind of quality work they are capable of doing.

For years, when a problem arose while I was teaching, I would tell my students what the solution to that problem would be, then expend great effort trying to get the students to accept my solution. I call this "My Way" to solve problems. It is a win-lose proposition—I would win and the students would lose. This model, shown below, depended on my ability to create a relationship based on rewards and punishment, fear and dependency. If the students resisted my solution, I would try to bribe them or threaten them to get them to go along. I used this approach for years, until I could not stand myself anymore. I was exhausted.

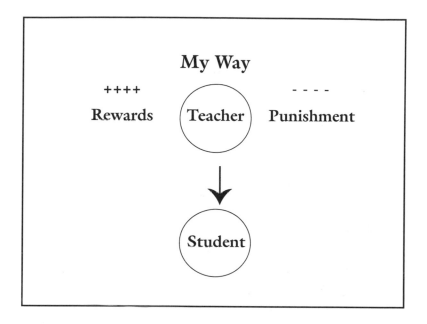

Then I moved to a permissive approach. I gave up my responsibility for solving problems. I asked the students how *they* would solve the problem, leaving out any input or ideas on my part. I call this "Their Way" to solve problems. It created a win-lose situation in which the students would win at my expense. With the My Way approach, students were left out of the process. Problem-solving was done *to* them. By comparison, with Their Way, I was left out of the process, and the solution was imposed on me.

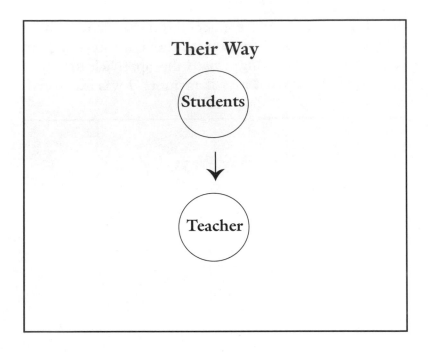

Their Way

Students

↓

Teacher

In either case, solving problems My Way or solving problems Their Way, one of the parties had no involvement in the mental creation of solutions, therefore no commitment to the physical creation—putting forth the effort to cooperate and make the solution work. I used this second approach until I could not stand the students anymore, at which point I jumped back to My Way of solving problems, until I became sick of myself and jumped back to Their Way, until I became sick of them, and so on. It became too frustrating for all of us.

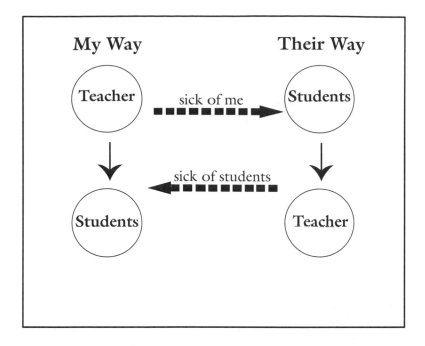

I figured there had to be a better way. I found the clues to Our Way in Stephen R. Covey's books, *Principle-Centered Leadership* (1992) and *The Seven Habits of Highly Effective People* (1989). Unlike My Way or Their Way, Our Way to solve problems is not based on a dominating, "power over" process, but rather it becomes a "power with" process. It is not based upon fear and dependency, rewards and punishment, nor on giving up responsibility as a teacher by allowing the students to decide what solutions shall be used. With Our Way the teacher makes the decision to share the responsibility to solve problems, involving students in the process while remaining involved as the teacher, so it becomes a cooperative way to solve conflicts.

Our Way is the best model I know of. It effectively creates involvement by empowering students and teachers to share in the mental creation of solutions, so everyone is committed to carrying out the solutions, the physical creation. The cooperative process by which teachers and students can solve problems I have characterized as the TORI PROCESS, an acronym that is explained in detail in Figure 6. A step-by-step, practical guide for lead managers to use for problem solving is presented in Figure 7. Let me give you an example of how the process can work.

As Apollo High School grew larger and needed more classrooms, we quickly built some prefab, portable buildings. The soundproofing in these buildings was not good. One was used by a music class where students played a piano, guitars, banjos, violins, and a harmonica. One day a student brought in a four-foot bongo drum. When he played the drum in the music class, it was heard in all the other prefab classrooms. Students and teachers complained about the noise.

A boss manager would probably have gone down to the class and blamed the students, taken the drum away, and threatened that if anyone did anything stupid like that again, the class would be canceled. But having adopted the principles of lead management, I realized that the students were not the problem. The problem was the noise coming from the drum in a classroom that did not have good soundproofing (a problem within the system). Talking with the students, I told them the noise coming from the drums was annoying and distracting others from learning. I told the class that I respected their needs, but I also respected the needs of other students, as well as my own. I asked, "Can we solve this problem in a way that no one is blamed, where one group does not win at the expense of the needs of another group? Can we solve this problem in such a way that we all win?" Using the problem-solving approach outlined in Figure 7, we began to search for solutions.

We eventually agreed that all the students and teachers in the building would bring in egg cartons, and when enough egg cartons had been collected the students would staple them on the four walls of the classroom and on the back of the door to serve as soundproofing. While the egg cartons were being collected, I would keep the bongo drum in my office. In less than one month, more than 3,000 egg cartons were brought in and the students stapled them up. When I gave them back the conga drum, and they played it, we could just barely hear it in the other classrooms.

What was most important was not that we solved the problem, but that in doing so we respected each other's needs and worked together to solve the problem with a win-win approach and without blaming. This was a quality solution and experience for all those involved. The foundation for this type of problem solving is to eliminate blaming and stimulus-response thinking, to understand our basic needs and control theory, and to work together to find quality solutions.

Figure 6
TORI PROCESS

1. TRUSTING	22. TEAM/TOGETHERNESS
↓	↑
2. OPENNESS	21. OWNERSHIP
↓	↑
3. RESPONSIVENESS	20. RESULTS
↓	↑
4. INTERDEPENDENT	19. INSIDE OUT
↓	↑
5. PROBLEMS	18. PROACTIVE
↓	↑
6. RESPONSIBLE	17. RELATIONSHIP
↓	↑
7. OPEN	16. ONGOING
↓	↑
8. COMMUNICATION	15. COMMITMENT
↓	↑
9. ENERGY	14. ENVIRONMENT
↓	↑
10. SOLUTIONS	13. SECURE
↓	↑
11. SATISFYING	12. SAFE
→	↑

Beginning with the upper left, and finishing at the upper right, the TORI PROCESS builds (1) *trust* to create (2) *openness* in our communication so we become (3) *responsive* to each other, and that creates an (4) *interdependent* relationship, allowing us to solve (5) *problems* in a (6) *responsible* way with (7) *open* and honest (8) *communication* that creates the (9) *energy* to find (10) *solutions* that are (11) *satisfying* to each person involved, students and teacher, by creating a (12) *safe*, (13) *secure*, friendly, and supportive (14) *environment* where each person is (15) *committed* to an (16) *ongoing*, growing (17) *relationship* that is (18) *proactive* rather then reactive, so problems are solved together from (19) the *inside out*, to get quality (20) *results*, so each of us feels (21) *ownership* because we were a part of the solution, instead of being blamed for being the problem, which creates the (22) *togetherness* one feels as a result of working as a *team*.

Figure 7
Six Steps to Lead Management Problem Solving

1. **Identifying or Defining the Problem**:
   What's my need?
   What's bothering me?
   What's the trouble?
   What's going wrong?

2. **Generating Alternative Solutions**:
   What might be done?
   What options do I have?
   What are some possible solutions?
   What might be tried?

3. **Evaluating the Solutions**:
   What are the advantages and disadvantages?
   What are the risks?
   What data do I have?

4. **Decision Making**:
   What is the best alternative?
   What feels right?
   What will minimize the risks?

5. **Implementation**:
   Who does what, and by when?

6. **Follow-Up Self-Evaluation**:
   How are things going?
   Did the decision solve the problem?

Chapter 9

From Evaluation by Others
to Concurrent and Self-Evaluation

A key element in becoming a quality school is teaching the students how to evaluate their own work. As the school moves towards quality, teachers and administrators, as well as classified employees, will also begin to evaluate their own work. As mentioned in Chapter 1, the steps that lead to quality are: focus on quality, eliminate coercion, and get students to evaluate their own work. Of these, self-evaluation is the most difficult for students—they resist this change more than any other. We must, however, convince them that self-evaluation is a skill that will help to improve the quality of their lives not only now, but forever. Students must look at their own work as they move towards quality, thinking of ways to improve it. Once they leave school, they are on their own—no teacher will be around to tell them if what they are doing is quality work.

One discussion that Dr. Glasser had with the Apollo students was particularly effective in getting them to see the importance of self-evaluation and doing quality work.

He asked if anybody had had surgery, and several students replied they had. He then asked them, "When you look for a doctor to perform your surgery, do you look for a C+ doctor? a B- surgeon? or do you look for a A+ surgeon? When you go to the dentist, are you looking for a B- dentist, or are you looking or a A+ dentist?" The point was well made. When we look for someone to provide us with a service, whether it is a health service, food service, or hotel service, we are looking for quality. Nobody wants to pay for a C meal or stay in a C hotel. This line of reasoning helped the students to see the value of doing their best. It also became clear to them that their first efforts were seldom their best. Quality usually comes with the second, third, or fourth effort as they continually work to improve their assignment. Students resist evaluating work that they perceive is irrelevant, however. Only when the work we ask them to do is meaningful will they exert themselves to do careful self-evaluations.

When Apollo students are ready to turn in their completed work, the teacher quickly scans the paper, then asks the student, "Is there any thing you can think of that you might change, delete, or add that would improve the quality of this paper?" A large percentage of our students have suggestions about how to improve the quality of their work. It turns out that all we have to do is ask. A small percentage, however, reply, "This is the best paper I've ever written. Aren't you ever going to be satisfied?" The teacher, who understands the student's frustration, agrees by saying, "Yes, this is one of the best papers that you have done for me. I'm curious though. If you were the teacher, what grade would you give it?" Most students say a B or B-. Then the teacher simply returns to the self-evaluation mode, asking the student, "What would you have to change or add to make it an A paper?" This usually gets the student to begin thinking again about how he or she might improve the assignments.

Numerous self-evaluation strategies can help students of all ages focus on the quality of their work. One is called "Where are you?" (Figure 8).

Figure 8
Where Are You?

The tree represents a classroom of students at the end of a quarter or the end of a particular unit. The teacher explains, "This is our class. The tree is the unit we have been studying for the last month. Think about how well you feel you understand the material. Looking at the tree, where do you see yourself?" Most students would like to be at the top of the tree. If they say they are only halfway up the tree, then they are perceiving they have not done their best. Using control theory, the teacher asks next, "What do you have to do to get from where you are to where you would like to be?" If students have difficulty answering this question, the teacher asks their permission to make some suggestions. "I have some ideas on how you might get closer to where you would like to be. Would you like to hear them?"

In Dr. Glasser's *The Quality School* (1990) there is a chapter about concurrent evaluation which introduces the acronym SESIR to stand for the process "Show me, Explain, Self-Evaluation, Improvement, Repeat." The first part of concurrent evaluation is *show me* what you have done, and then *explain* to me how you did it. To prompt students for explanations as they show their work you can ask such questions as: Can you explain how it was done? What research did you do? Did you go to the library or interview any one? How did you organize your thoughts? The third part of concurrent evaluation is implementing *self-evaluation* . As the students explain how they did the work, you can ask some leading questions to help them improve the quality of their work. For example, suppose in a term paper a student had made several references, but did not include a bibliography or footnotes. You could point out to the student that the work would be more accurate and of higher quality if sources were identified. The next part of concurrent evaluation is based on *improvement*. How could the student's work be improved?

What changes could be made? Once those improvements are made, the student will *repeat* the process. Show, explain, self-evaluate, improve, and repeat the process. The more often this is done with students, the more they will internalize the process, and the more effective they will become at evaluating their own work.

The second self-evaluation strategy, "Which One Are You and Why?" (Figure 9), is based on our knowledge that quality always feels good. We have a sense of pride when we do the best work that we can.

Figure 9

Which One Are You And Why?

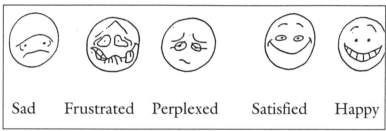

Sad   Frustrated   Perplexed   Satisfied   Happy

Using this strategy, the teacher asks the students to look at the five faces and pick the one that best represents how they feel about the work they have just completed. If the student points out any face other than the one on the far right, which signifies that he is very happy and satisfied with what he has done, then the teacher goes through the concurrent evaluation process described above. The teacher asks the student what could be done to improve the project so he would be able to experience a really happy feeling.

A simple strategy, called the Self-Evaluation Scale (Figure 10), is a scale from 1 to 10—1 representing poor quality and 10 representing excellence. The student is asked to locate where on the scale he judges the quality of his work to be.

Figure 10
Self-Evaluation Scale

Workmanship

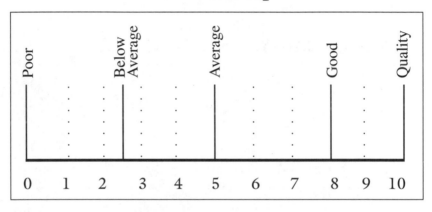

A particularly effective self-evaluation form used by an Apollo High School teacher is presented in Figure 11. Of course, students must first be taught the self-evaluation skills that make the use of this form beneficial. This particular teacher modeled the self-evaluation process by sharing with her students how she constantly evaluated the lessons she prepared, revised them, and improved them. She sought feedback from her students as to their perceptions of the lessons and how they would improve them. She taught by example and understood the importance of not hurrying, gently introducing her students to the self-evaluation process. She did concurrent evaluation with them and also had students work in small groups with opportunities to experiment with peer evaluation. In the safe, trusting environment of her classroom, feedback, suggestion, improvement and self-evaluation were welcomed, not something to be afraid of.

Figure 11

INDIVIDUAL EVALUATION

[Feel free to make your own modifications to adapt to your particular purpose.]

1. What I liked best about this learning experience was: _____

2. What I least understood about this assignment, and something I need to spend more time on so I'll better understand, is: _____

3. One way this learning experience could have been better was:_____

4. My basic needs include power, fun, freedom, and love or belonging. The need that was most met through this learning experience was _____ because:_____
   _____
   _____
   _____
   _____

The need which was least met was the need for
_____, which could be met better the next
time if we would:_____

5. Three ways I could use what I learned from this
   experience in my life, are:
   1._____
   2._____
   3._____

6. If I were the teacher in this class, one thing I
   would have done that would have improved the
   quality of this assignment would be: _____

7. For me the overall rating I would give this learning experience on the scale below would be:
            0 1 2 3 4 5 6 7 8 9 10 (circle your #)
        poor   average   great

Many primary-grade teachers seem to understand
readily the important aspects of self-evaluation. Most do
not give traditional report cards with letter grades to students in grades K through 3. They give progress reports.
The teachers usually focus first on things the student is
doing well. They build on the students' strengths before
they make suggestions for improvement. When feedback
is given after the students are asked to self-evaluate, they are
usually more willing to accept suggestions for improvement.

At Colbert Elementary School (Mead, Washington) students attend parent/teacher conferences and in

eighteen of the twenty-eight classrooms they actually lead the conferences, based on portfolios they have compiled. Parents are often surprised at how valuable this experience can be. For instance, when Sally and her parents arrived for a late-fall conference, the teacher noticed that Sally, a good student, looked as if she had been crying. The teacher asked if it would be better to reschedule the conference. Before Sally could answer, her father said sternly, "No, let's get this over with." The mother followed quietly.

Sally introduced her parents to the teacher and sat on one side of the table. She asked her parents to sit across from her while the teacher took a seat at one end. Very quickly Sally took out three folders and a stack of index cards. She started by explaining that she was going to show her parents examples of what she had been doing at the beginning of the school year, followed by examples showing how she had improved in the last three months. She said that she would then share her plans for showing more improvement in a few areas where she thought she could have done better. She also explained that she would be discussing some of her behaviors in school and how proud she was about learning to make changes when things were not going as well as she thought they should.

Without hesitation she started the process by bringing out a folder with samples of writing from the beginning of the year and at various times since. As she went along she pointed out what she felt were her improvements. She followed the writings with a list of books she had read and explained how some of her writing ideas had come from some of the books. As she started on her math papers she explained that she likes math, but she didn't think she was putting as much time into it as she would like. She reached over to the pile of index cards and began to share a plan for math homework she wanted to try.

At that moment her father said softly, "Time out, Sally. I have to tell your teacher something." To the teacher he said, "The reason Sally looked the way she did when we came in was because I had been yelling at her about how ridiculous it was for an eleven-year-old to evaluate her own work. I told her this was a waste of all our time and I was going to tell you that. My wife told me to be nice and give it a chance because Sally seems to be enjoying school this year." To his daughter he continued, "Sally, I was wrong, and if your teacher will take the time to help me, maybe I could try some of this with the eighth-grade math class I teach." The teacher looked the father in the eye and said, "I am sorry that I may not have enough time to help you, but I am sure Sally does."

Staff at Francis Reh Elementary School (Saginaw, Michigan) decided to extend student self-evaluations to their annual awards ceremony. Many schools end the year or a semester with an awards ceremony at which certain students, selected by the staff, are rewarded with certificates, ribbons or prizes for good citizenship, progress, achievement, attendance, and other behaviors. At Francis Reh School, however, the students themselves are asked what they consider to be their most improved area, the work they are most proud of, or something they learned and did a good job at that is important to them.

At their assembly in June 1993, the self-evaluations were read by the students and they were recognized for their achievements. Some of the things students shared were: "I'm proud of myself because last year I was afraid to enter class discussions, and this year I'm really trying to say more." "I haven't been in a fight all year—I'm trying to find better ways to solve problems." "I read 100 books without being told to. It was my choice." "I've been helping kindergarten students to improve their work." During the reading of accomplishments, spontaneous applause burst forth for all students, something that had never happened before. Overall there was a much higher level of involvement, celebration and pride. For the first time, no crumpled, discarded awards littered the floor or filled the trash cans.

Self-evaluation is as important for teachers as it is for students. In the past I visited teachers once or twice a school year and then filled out the standardized evaluation form on their performance, going over it with them without any real involvement or input on their part. The teacher would sign the evaluation, I would sign it, and then it was sent to the district office to be added to the personnel files. As my understanding of control theory grew, I wondered how such minimal observations could determine the areas in which a teacher needed to improve. How could a teacher's strengths be determined within such a short evaluation time? I realized that the teachers knew more accurately than I did what they were doing well and what they needed to improve on.

So I asked the teachers to complete the evaluation form themselves and then to make an appointment with me to sit down and go over it. At our meeting I asked the teachers to identify four or five things they were experiencing success with on their job, which I would reinforce, and then I added two or three observations of my own. Next I would ask the teacher to share one or two things that they were working on to improve, and ask if I could do anything to help them to get to where they wanted to be. The staff reported to me that this was one of the most valuable evaluation procedures that they had ever experienced in public education.

Administrators who evaluate teachers should make the evaluation process one which improves the performance of teaching. Many times teachers are afraid to share some of the areas in which they need improvement, because they believe it will be used against them. They fear it could become part of their personnel file and thus a tool for possible dismissal. This is not the purpose of evaluation. It is to improve teaching and managing. The same principles apply to an administrator evaluating a teacher as to the teacher evaluating a student. If the administrator focuses first on the things that a teacher does well, the teacher will be more comfortable about sharing some things he or she is having difficulty with, so there can be a dialogue to assist in planning how to improve.

One teacher I worked with considered herself unsuccessful with cooperative-learning experiences. I asked if she knew of anything that might help her to be more successful in the future. She told me that she would really like to observe another teacher on our staff who seemed to be very successful with cooperative learning. "When this teacher uses cooperative learning," she said, "her students are still talking about what they have learned when they come into my class. They are so excited about it." We agreed she should talk with that teacher and request to observe her next cooperative-learning assignment. I agreed to arrange to have her class covered so she could take advantage of this experience. After observing the cooperative-learning assignment, she and the other teacher could sit down together and talk about what she had observed.

This is the true purpose of evaluation in education—helping people to improve the quality of their teaching. It has not been done this way in many schools, but it is something that can be learned. It must be applied in our schools if we are to move teachers toward quality teaching.

Principals who are lead managers will talk about the importance of self-evaluation. They will give teachers opportunities to share their successes in self-evaluation. They will encourage teachers to share some of the strategies they have created and experiences they have had, so they can learn from each other. When teachers see effective, successful teaching methods and strategies that others have used, it builds a sense of pride and a sense of cohesiveness among staff members.

NEW PARADIGMS FOR CREATING QUALITY SCHOOLS

Chapter 10

Other Significant Paradigms and Putting it All Together

The previous chapters have described what I consider the essential paradigm shifts for creating quality schools. As a school staff begins its journey to quality, however, other significant paradigm shifts occur. In my experience, these spring forth once the key paradigms are in place.

From Innate Ability to Effort

No longer should there be emphasis upon the innate ability of students. The effort that students put forth as they try to learn skills should be paramount. Effort involves concentration, practice, repetition. Ultimately, it leads to improvement in quality. Students' skills inevitably progress if they are willing to expend effort to improve those skills. The level at which they start is much less important than the level that they finally reach.

From Input to Output

There should be less concern about filling students' minds with lots of input—lectures, worksheets, learning packets—and more concern about specific, desired outcomes. Students must be able to demonstrate their knowledge in the form of skills. What counts in a quality school is not remembering knowledge, but using knowledge to improve our lives and the lives of others.

From Rote Learning to Mastery

No longer are students expected merely to memorize and repeat information, only to forget it as soon as they have been tested. In quality schools, students must master certain skills which all perceive to be worthy of the investment of time and energy. By mastering these skills, students can improve the way they live and interact with others.

From Seat Time to Achievement

Students should no longer serve seat time for a semester or a year, then be passed on to the next subject or grade level. When they demonstrate their skills to the satisfaction of the teacher, they should move on to the next level. It is not a matter of time but a matter of discovering that learning adds quality to our lives. When students at Apollo demonstrated their skills, many of them received full credit without serving the normal seat time, but then became teacher's assistants. They helped the teachers by working with other students, which not only helped those students learn even better, but also helped the teacher's assistants themselves deepen their understanding and sharpen their skills.

From Lecturer to Manager

This was one of the most difficult paradigm shifts for teachers and administrators at Apollo to make as we moved to becoming a quality school. We needed to learn new skills to convince students that what is worth learning is worth learning well. Students learn more of what they are involved with than what they are simply told about, and facilitators and managers are much more successful at getting people involved than lecturers are.

From Objective Tests to Authentic Assessment

A machine can never score a quality experience. New methods must be developed to assess what students have learned in a quality school. Demonstrations of skill which involve self-evaluation are required. Performances, exhibitions, and portfolios are examples of authentic assessment tools. We have a long way to go in this area, but it is a most important process.

From Time Periods to Flexible Scheduling

We are beginning to see more effective scheduling than traditional fifty-minute periods. Block scheduling; academic classes on Monday, Wednesday, and Friday with elective classes in longer periods on Tuesday and Thursday; students taking core classes for two and three hours, while taking other classes for shorter periods; students learning off-campus in the community as well as in school; classes offered in the late afternoons and evenings, as well as during the day. Possibilities abound. All it takes are people who are committed to try something different and perhaps more effective than what they are currently doing.

From "It's Good Enough"
to Continuous Improvement

Quality schools understand that quality is a journey, not a destination. The excitement is in the *going* there, rather than the *arriving* there. It is a continuous-improvement process, the key to which is self-evaluation.

From Superintendent as Dictator
to Superintendent as Choreographer

In a quality school district, no longer is there dictatorial, top-down management. No longer does one person create the vision and the rules. A quality school district is led by a superintendent who knows the importance of involvement to create commitment. The superintendent becomes a facilitator, cheerleader, coach, visionary, one who "begins with the end in mind and puts first things first."

From Education Being Only the School's Business
to Education Being Everyone's Business

Quality schools involve the entire community in educating a child. Staff, students, parents, citizens, and business people will all play a role, supporting each other instead of blaming each other. Only *together* can we make a real difference.

From School Board's Responsibility to Provide
Leadership to School Board's Responsibility
to See that Leadership Is Provided

The responsibility of a quality school board is to establish policy and hire lead managers who know how to work with people to bring out the best in them. In too many school districts, it is "us against them," a "power over" approach that prevents schools from becoming quality by its very nature. We must have leaders who understand that "power with" leads to "power within," so quality can be experienced by staff and students.

From I, Me, and Mine to We, Us, and Our

No longer will one group decide what another group should do, then stand over them to make sure they get it done—not administrators over teachers, teachers over students, teachers over parents, parents over teachers, board members over superintendent, or superintendent over site administrators. Quality develops from sharing the viewpoint of "We, Us, Our." Leaders within a school system create quality with a team approach.

From Textbooks as the Focus of Learning to Process as the Focus of Learning

Quality teachers do not rely on textbooks as their main source of learning. Learning under a quality teacher involves more hands-on, group process, and application opportunities. Textbooks will only be a supplement to learning in the community, skill building, problem solving, critical thinking, accessing information and technology, etc.

From Reactive to Proactive

Personnel in a quality school will stop the practice of putting out small fires, reacting to the few individuals who complain, thus allowing them to determine the agenda. They will deal with causes of problems through effective communication and problem-solving techniques. They will empower the large majority who want to help improve our schools, not just stand back and complain. They will point out where things are right, rather than focusing on what is wrong, and celebrate successes without worrying about who gets the credit.

Many educators are familiar with Dr. Deming's points that lead to quality and with Dr. Covey's seven habits of effective leadership and the seven principles upon which these seven habits are based. These two distinguished educators describe in very specific ways some of the behaviors and concerns of lead managers. Dr. Glasser describes why Dr. Deming's fourteen points and Dr. Covey's habits and principles actually work. People tend not to change until they understand *why* they should change. Dr. Glasser teaches people how to manage others in such a way that they become motivated from within, based on their internal, basic needs and self-evaluation, thereby creating the involvement and ownership required to change. This is the control theory, an inside-out process compared to the futile efforts of trying to coerce people to make changes, which is a stimulus-response, outside-in process.

There are many programs available to administrators and teachers, such as clinical instruction and mastery learning, outcome-based education, cooperative learning and team learning, various basic skills curricula, model curriculum programs, integrated curriculum programs and others. All of these programs have good ideas and new approaches to help students learn more effectively. But how do you manage people in such a way that they are convinced that implementing these various programs is worth the time and energy they will put into the process? If real change comes from within, how do managers lead people to come to the decision that they want to make these changes?

Dr. Glasser's teachings invite people to consider all of the paradigms mentioned in this book. People adopt these paradigms and choose to change because they see the benefits of change, not only in themselves, but in those they lead and manage.

Let me summarize some of the principles that teachers who desire to be "quality teacher/managers" will practice in their teaching. Quality teachers will move from a concern for what they are going to teach to focusing on what is worth learning. These teachers will realize that if students are not learning the way they teach, they need to teach the way the students learn. Quality teachers will always explain why the assignments or learning particular material may be useful to the students now and in the future and how in some way it will add quality to their lives and perhaps the lives of others. Quality teachers will use a variety of methods, knowing that students do not all learn the same things in the same way at the same time. As much as possible they will convert the knowledge they want students to learn to specific skills such as writing, speaking, or calculating, so students can actually demonstrate their skill.

Quality teachers will teach students how to evaluate and improve their own work—an essential skill for the

21st century. In the work force, when someone makes a mistake or a poor effort, people are less interested in excuses or punishments than in how the worker can make it right. Students should be taught this first in school so it can be transferred to work situations. Quality teachers will always give students an opportunity to improve their work, instead of giving scores or grades that are forever fixed. Quality teachers have high expectations for their students because they believe that under the right conditions students can do better work than they are now doing.

Quality teachers will see the importance of using group processes, such as cooperative learning, in their teaching. They realize that students learn the most when they teach something to others, so peer tutoring will be practiced in a quality classroom. Quality teachers will work at improving the system instead of blaming the students, parents, or administrators for the problems they face. They will spend their time and energy where they can make a difference, not trying to change something over which they have no control.

Quality teachers will have few discipline problems because in their classroom students will be meeting their basic needs. The antidote for discipline problems is not punishment, but useful curriculum and quality teaching. Quality teachers hear statements from student such as: "Miss Taylor makes history interesting. I see how what happened in history is really related to what is happening in the world today." "I like this class because we can ask questions and my teacher really listens and values our opinions." "For the first time I'm really enjoying science. We do a lot of hands-on experiments to see why things work the way they do." "In Mrs. Brown's class we get to work in groups some of the time, and I like that." "Mrs. Smith spends more time on telling us what we did right instead of what we did wrong. That makes me want to work harder." "Mrs. Fernandez really believes I have something to offer, and that makes me want to work hard and prove she's right."

Poor discipline and behavior problems are more common in classrooms where students ask, "Why do we have to learn this?" and the teacher answers, "Because it will be on the test," or "Because I told you to," or "Someday you'll understand why—for now, just do it." The same teachers also tend to make comments such as, "You'll never get a good job as long as you have that kind of attitude." "Do I have to send you to the office or call your parents, or will you do what I ask you to do?" "You can do the work now or after school." "You are just lazy and always find an excuse not to work." "Why can't you work as well as the other students?" Such statements are heard in boss-managed classrooms where students resist instead of co-operate. The boss-like teacher spends time and energy trying to force students to obey rather than on effective ways to teach useful skills.

When teachers everywhere realize their biggest and most difficult job is managing students, when they see how students are motivated from within because of their basic needs, that using coercion does not make things better, that all meaningful and lasting change comes from within, that when we try to solve problems Our Way we have win-win solutions, when they listen to students instead of lecture to them, when they abandon finding fault and seek to find solutions that everyone can feel good about, when they move away from competition towards cooperation and teamwork, when they work to build and maintain trust so students know they really care, and when they know the importance of continually improving and finding new ways to reach their students, then there will be quality schools everywhere, instead of just a few here and there. I wish you much success as you begin your never-ending journey to quality, the only journey worth taking in education.

Afterword

The schools listed below, with which I have worked during the past several years, have enriched my understanding of quality-school principles and my appreciation for what can be accomplished by dedicated, innovative individuals. Their contributions to this book have been immeasurable. I hope you have learned from me, and from them, some new ideas that will help launch your school in the direction of quality. I wish you the very best on your journey.

Bear River High School
Grant Conway
11130 Magnolia Road
Grass Valley, CA 95949
(916) 268-3700

Sierra Mountain High School
Earl Conway
12238 McCourtney Road
Grass Valley, CA 95945
(916) 272-2635

Hanalie School
Nick Beck
P.O. Box 46
Hanalie, Kauai, HI 96714
(808) 826-6266
Fax (808) 826-4122

Averill Career Opportunities Center
Julie Walker, Principal
2102 Weiss St.
Saginaw, MI 48602
(517) 797-4836

Brady Elementary
Dave Peterson, Principal
17295 Hemlock Road
Oakley, MI 48649
(517) 845-7060

Carrollton Elementary School
Mark Jaremba, Principal
P.O. Box 517
Carrollton, MI 48724
(517) 754-2425

Francis Reh Academy
Kathy Hugo, Principal
2201 Owen St.
Saginaw, MI 48601
(517) 753-2349

Plainfield Elementary School
Jane Van Steenis
2775 Shattuck Road
Saginaw, MI 48603

Saginaw County Business/Education
Coordinating Council
Kathy Conklin, Executive Director
901 South Washington St.
Saginaw, MI 48601
(517) 752-7161

Edin Prairie Schools
Gerald McCoy, Superintendent
8100 School Road
Edin Prairie, MN 55344-2292
(612) 937-1650
Fax (612) 937-3665

South View Middle School
Kathryn M. Dockter
4725 South View Lane
Edina, MN 55424
(612) 928-2700

Copperas Cove High School
W.L. Sanders, Principal
400 South 25th St.
P.O. Box 58
Copperas Cove, TX 76522
(817) 547-2534

E.L. Kent Elementary
Carrollton-Farmers Branch Indpt. School District
1800 West Rosemeade Parkway
Carrollton, TX 75007
(214) 323-6464
Fax (214)-323-6455

Ingram Independent School District
Mary Ward
700 Highway 39
Ingram, TX 78025
(512) 367-5517
Fax (512) 367-4869

Newman Smith High School
Carrollton-Farmers Branch Indpt. School District
2335 North Josey Lane
Carrollton, TX 75006
(214) 323-5800
Fax (214) 323-5866

Robert E. Lee High School
Eddie Milham, Principal
411 East Loop 323
Tyler, TX 75701
(903) 531-3900
Fax (903) 531-3994

Colbert Elementary
Jerry Johnson
Conn Wittwer
Rt. 3 Box 94
Colbert, WA 99005
(509) 468-3028

Washougal High School
Ed Fitts
1201 39th Street
Washougal, WA 98671
(206) 835-2155

Platte County School District #1
Merle Smith
13th and Oak Street
Wheatland, WY 82201
(307) 322-2075
Fax (307) 322-2084

I would enjoy hearing from you about other paradigms that you have used or heard about which would help in creating a quality school.

> Bradley H. Greene
> Self-Esteem and the Quality School
> An Educational Consultant Service
> 938 Rivera Street
> Simi Valley, CA 93065
> (805) 527-5291
> Fax (805) 584-3314

References
and Recommended
Readings

Bailey, William. *School-Site Management Applied*. Lancaster, PA: Technomic Pub. Co., 1991.

Block, Peter. *The Empowered Manager: Positive Political Skills at Work*. San Francisco: Jossey-Bass, 1987.

Bloom, Benjamin S., George F. Madaus, and J. Thomas Hastings. *Evaluation To Improve Learning*. New York: McGraw-Hill, 1981.

Boffey, Barnes. *Reinventing Yourself*. Chapel Hill, NC: New View Publications, 1993.

Buscaglia, Leo F. *Living, Loving and Learning*. New York: Holt, Rinehart and Winston, 1982.

Carducci, Dewey. *The Caring Classroom: A Guide for Teachers Troubled by the Difficult Student and Classroom Disruption*. Palo Alto, CA: Bull Publishing Co., 1984.

Covey, Stephen R. *The Seven Habits of Highly Effective*

People: Restoring the Character Ethic. New York: Simon & Schuster, 1989.

_____. *Principle-Centered Leadership.* New York: Summit Books, 1991.

Deming, W. Edwards. *The New Economics for Industry, Government, Education.* Cambridge, MA: Massachusetts Institute of Technology, 1993.

De Pree, Max. *Leadership Is an Art.* East Lansing, MI: Michigan University Press, 1987.

Dobyns, Lloyd. *Quality or Else: The Revolution in World Business.* Boston: Houghton Mifflin, 1991.

_____. *Thinking about Quality: Progress, Wisdom and the Deming Philosophy.* New York: Times Books/Random House, 1994.

Dyer, Wayne. *Pulling Your Own Strings.* New York: T. Y. Crowell Co., 1978.

Gabor, Andrea. *The Man Who Discovered Quality: How W. Edwards Deming Brought the Quality Revolution to America.* New York: Random House, 1990.

Ginott, Haim G. *Teacher and Child: A Book for Parents and Teachers.* New York: McMillan, 1972.

Glasser, William. *Reality Therapy.* New York: HarperCollins, 1965.

_____. *Schools Without Failure*. New York: Harper-Collins, 1969.

_____. *Control Theory*. New York: HarperCollins, 1984.

_____. *Control Theory in the Classroom*. New York: HarperCollins, 1986.

_____. *The Quality School*. New York: HarperCollins, 1990.

_____. *The Quality School Teacher*. New York: HarperCollins, 1993.

_____. *The Control Theory Manager*. New York: HarperCollins, 1994.

Good, Perry. *In Pursuit of Happiness*. Chapel Hill, NC: New View Publications, 1987.

_____. *Helping Kids Help Themselves*. Chapel Hill, NC: New View Publications, 1992.

Gossen, Diane. *Restitution*. Chapel Hill, NC: New View Publications, 1993.

Greene, Brad. *Self Esteem and the Quality School*. Quality Training, 938 Rivera Street, Simi Valley, CA 93065.

Johnson, David W., Roger T. Johnson, Edith J. Holubec,

and Patricia Roy. *Circles of Learning: Cooperation in the Classroom.* Alexandria, VA: Association for Supervision and Curriculum Development, 1984.

Johnson, LouAnne. *My Posse Don't Do Homework.* New York: St. Martin's Press, 1992.

Kohn, Alfie. *No Contest: The Case Against Competition.* Boston: Houghton Mifflin, 1987.

Leonhardt, Mary. *Parents Who Love Reading, Kids Who Don't: How It Happens and What You Can Do about It.* New York: Crown Publishers/Random House, 1993.

Lepper, Mark R., and David Greene, eds. *The Hidden Costs of Reward: New Perspectives on the Psychology of Human Motivation.* Hillsdale, NJ: L. Erlbaum Assoc., 1978.

McNeil, Linda. *Contradictions of Control: School Structure and School Knowledge.* New York: Routledge and K. Paul, 1986.

Olson, Ken. *The Art of Hanging Loose in an Uptight World: Featuring Psychological Exercises for Personal Growth.* New York: Simon & Schuster, 1974.

Orsburn, Jack D., Linda Moran, Ed Musselwhite, Joan H. Zenger, with Craig Perrin. *Self-Directed Work Teams: The New American Challenge.* Homewood, IL: Business One Irwin, 1990.

Ryan, Kathleen, and Daniel K. Oestreich. *Driving Fear Out of the Workplace: How to Overcome the Invisible Barriers to Quality, Productivity, and Innovation*. San Francisco: Jossey-Bass, 1991.

Stevenson, Harold W., and James W. Stigler. *The Learning Gap: Why Our Schools Are Failing and What We Can Learn from Japanese and Chinese Education*. New York: Summit Books, 1992.

Sullo, Robert. *Teach Them To Be Happy*. Chapel Hill, NC: New View Publications, 1989.

Tinsley, Mariwyn, and Mona Perdue. *The Journey to Quality*. Chapel Hill, NC: New View Publications, 1992.

All self evaluation strategies and the TORI PROCESS problem-solving model were created by the author.

True Colors. Corona, CA: True Colors Communications Group, 1987

Petals. Chapel Hill, NC: New View Publications, 1992